DEVELOPING A RESEARCH PROGRAM
IN HUMAN SERVICE AGENCIES

DEVELOPING A RESEARCH PROGRAM IN HUMAN SERVICE AGENCIES

A Practitioner's Guidebook

By

DENNIS H. REID, PH.D.

Habilitative Management Consultants, Inc.
and
Western Carolina Center
Morganton, North Carolina

CHARLES C THOMAS • PUBLISHER
Springfield • Illinois • U.S.A.

Published and Distributed Throughout the World by

CHARLES C THOMAS • PUBLISHER

2600 South First Street

Springfield, Illinois 62794-9265

© *1987 by* CHARLES C THOMAS • PUBLISHER

ISBN 0-398-05349-9

Library of Congress Catalog Card Number: 87-6531

With THOMAS BOOKS *careful attention is given to all details of manufacturing and
design. It is the Publisher's desire to present books that are satisfactory as to their physical
qualities and artistic possibilities and appropriate for their particular use.* THOMAS
BOOKS *will be true to those laws of quality that assure a good name and good will.*

Printed in the United States of America
Q-R-3

Library of Congress Cataloging in Publication Data

Reid, Dennis H.
  Developing a research program in human service
agencies.

  Bibliography: p.
  Includes index.
  1. Social service — Research — Handbooks,
manuals, etc. I. Title.
HV11.R386   1987   361'.0072   87-6531
ISBN 0-398-05349-9

To Helen, Cason and Nate

PREFACE

THE DEGREE to which human service agencies fulfill their designated mission of helping people in need is, in essence, dependent on the diligence and competence with which human service staff perform their work. Consequently, if improvements in service delivery systems are to take place, then human service staff must find ways to improve the effectiveness of their work activities. One major means of helping to bring about improvements in the human services is applied research. Applied research represents a method of enhancing the helping professions by developing new therapeutic technologies with empirically substantiated effectiveness as well as by refining and improving existing technologies. However, the overwhelming majority of applied research undertakings in the human services do not integrally involve the people who are responsible for providing those services. Rather, research endeavors are usually conducted by college- or university-based researchers. The lack of involvement of (human service) staff in research is a primary reason that many applied research projects that successfully lead to a published journal article on how to improve an aspect of human service provision do not significantly improve the routine operations of the respective human service agencies in which the research was conducted.

An underlying contention of this text is that if applied research is to truly enhance human service delivery, then staff who are responsible for delivering the services should be the individuals who conduct the research. The purpose of this text is to describe *how* personnel employed in human service agencies can conduct and publish applied research while simultaneously fulfilling their human service mission. By integrally involving human service practitioners in the design, implementation and dissemination of applied research, then the long-standing gap between state-of-the-art human service technology as reflected in the professional literature and what exists in the routine operations of most human service agencies can be eliminated or significantly reduced.

In describing how human service practitioners can successfully conduct applied research while at the same time provide services to clients, the focus will be on the _practical_ aspects of developing and maintaining a program of research. In this regard, the relative lack of involvement of human service staff in applied research activities is viewed not as a lack of research skill among practitioners (particularly professionals trained and/or experienced in applied behavior analysis or behavior modification) but, rather, as an inability of many practitioners to synthesize research undertakings into the operating characteristics of applied settings. Hence, workable strategies for incorporating research activities into routine job situations in human service settings will be emphasized.

Although this text is singularly authored, a number of people have had a significant impact on its development. In particular, the many competent clinicians, supervisors and administrators with whom I have had the opportunity to collaborate on applied research endeavors deserve considerable credit. The number of past and current colleagues is far too large to permit individual recognition here. However, many of their contributions are exemplified in the references throughout this text to their published research. In addition, special appreciation is extended to Helen Reid and Carole McNew for assistance in preparing the manuscript, to Carolyn Green and Terry Page for supporting the initial idea for the book, and to Carolyn Green, Marsha Parsons and Helen Reid for reviewing earlier drafts of the text.

D. R.

CONTENTS

DEVELOPING A RESEARCH PROGRAM
IN HUMAN SERVICE AGENCIES

Chapter 1

THE IMPORTANCE OF PRACTITIONERS CONDUCTING RESEARCH IN HUMAN SERVICE SETTINGS

A N IMPORTANT element in the design and improvement of human service programs is experimental research. Research represents the impetus for making the advances in therapeutic technologies that are continuously needed within the helping professions. In particular, results of research activities form an empirical basis with which to compare and evaluate newly developed approaches to therapy. In essence, research provides the human service professions with a scientific foundation for direction; without the objective data base that is generated by research, the helping professions are restricted to subjective speculation to guide their service delivery.

Historically, there have been two major types of research related to the human services: basic and applied. Basic research focuses on the development and refinement of theories of animal and human behavior. In this regard, basic research typically does not emphasize methods of improving human services; rather, the focus of basic research is on methods of understanding the functioning of organisms. In contrast, applied research focuses directly on methods of immediately improving aspects of human service programs. Of course, a symbiotic relationship is assumed to exist between basic and applied research, in that as the understanding of organismic functioning improves (basic research), the information gained can be used to foster improvements in the helping professions (applied research).

In the 1960s, a major advancement occurred in the relationship between research and the provision of human services. Prior to (and since) that time, a highly influential approach to basic research was the experimental analysis of behavior (see *Journal of the Experimental Analysis of*

Behavior, vol. 1-46). During the 1960s, an applied offshoot of the experimental analysis of behavior was developed: applied behavior analysis. Applied behavior analysis set the occasion for an unprecedented growth in both the quantity and quality of applied research in the human services.

Applied Behavior Analysis and Applied Research

Applied behavior analysis represents an approach to research in the human services (as well as other systems) that focuses on using principles of human behavior derived from the laboratory research of the experimental analysis of behavior. It is *applied,* in that it targets problems of immediate social significance for resolution. It is *behavioral,* in that its primary emphasis is on *changing human behavior.* It involves *analysis,* in that it identifies functional relationships between environmental events and changes in behavior — it identifies controlling variables over human behavior (cf. Baer, Wolf & Risley, 1968).

Due primarily to the focus of applied behavior analysis on topics of current social significance, the primary setting in which behavior analysis research is conducted is different from that of traditional research. Traditionally, the primary environment in which research has been conducted is the university-based laboratory. In contrast, with the advent of applied behavior analysis, the setting for applied research has become the normal environment in which human services are delivered. Such environments include school classrooms, institutional living units for the mentally retarded, nursing homes, community mental health clinics, general hospitals, preschools, psychiatric hospitals, sheltered workshops — essentially every location in which human service delivery systems exist. Because of the change in settings in which applied behavior analysis research occurs, the primary professionals who have historically conducted research (i.e. university faculty) have had to change their mode of operation. In particular, researchers have had to leave the laboratory on the university campus and become involved in existing human service agencies. This change in research settings and mode of operation for university researchers, although undoubtedly very successful in many ways, has generated some serious problems.

The problems involved in university-based researchers conducting their investigations in human service agencies are severalfold. First, because the vast majority of human service agencies do not include research as part of their primary mission, the researcher and the agency staff have different goals in terms of their purpose for functioning within the agency: the researcher is in the agency to do research, whereas agency staff are there to provide client services. Although research can certainly be directed at improving client sevices, there nevertheless is a substantial difference between activities focusing solely on client services and activities involved in various types of research projects. Where people working within one setting have different missions to fulfill, conflicts often arise. A second problem with university-based personnel conducting research in a human service agency is that because the researcher is an employee exclusively or primarily for the university and spends most of his/her time at the university campus in contrast to the human service agency, the researcher usually is not very knowledgeable regarding the day-to-day workings of the agency and its staff. When people (i.e. researchers) attempt to work within a setting with which they are not very knowledgeable, problems usually develop. Third, due in large part to the fact that the researcher is not a part of the agency's working population, he/she often has difficulty obtaining sufficient control of agency resources and/or management contingencies that are necessary to conduct a successful program of research.

The problems with university-based researchers conducting applied behavioral research in human service settings will be expanded on later in this text. However, the discussion on problems with this process is not meant to detract from the outstanding advances that have been made by university-based, applied behavior analysis researchers. University researchers have really been responsible for the bulk of the development and growth of applied behavior analysis. Unfortunately, though, the advances that have occurred to date have been more in the the development of the academic discipline of applied behavior analysis than in the human service agencies in which the research has been conducted. Although applied behavior analysis focuses on resolving problems of social significance through research, most behavior analysis research projects have not resulted in a thorough resolution of an existing problem in a human service agency. Typically, applied research projects conducted by university-based researchers only *demonstrate* how to solve a problem — and often under rather special circumstances arranged within a given agency. For various reasons, including those noted in the preceding paragraph, results of behavior analysis demonstration projects usually are not subsequently used by the agency in which the research was conducted to thoroughly resolve the targeted problem. Indeed, as discussed elsewhere (Liberman, 1983), the impact of many applied research projects on the functioning of the agencies in which the research was conducted usually lasts only as long as the formal research project, with all impact being lost even by the time the results of the project are published by the researcher.

An Alternative Approach to Research in Human Service Settings: Agency Staff Conducting Research in Their Own Agency

Due to the problems just noted as well as others that will be highlighted later, an alternative approach to conducting applied research in human service settings is warranted. One such alternative is for an agency's own staff to conduct applied research within their agency in contrast to relying on a researcher who is external to the human service agency. A number of advantages exist with this alternative. In particular, the three problems just noted with university-based personnel conducting research in applied settings are eliminated, or at least greatly diminished in severity. Also, because of the relatively tremendous growth in applied behavior analysis since the early 1960s, many human service agencies currently employ one or more professional staff members who are trained and experienced in behavior analysis and, consequently, have the core of technical skills necessary to conduct good applied research. For the most part, personnel with prerequisite applied research skills were not employed by typical human service agencies prior to the evolvement of applied behavior analysis.

An additional, and perhaps most important, advantage of agency staff being involved in applied research is that if agency personnel conduct the research in their own settings, it is much more likely that the benefits of the research will exist not only in the advancement of the professional discipline of applied behavior analysis but also for the human service agency, itself. In short, the *applied* purpose of applied behavior analysis is much more likely to be fulfilled if agency staff conduct the research that is intended to enhance their agency's services.

The primary reason that applied research conducted by staff in a human service agency is more likely to benefit the agency than research conducted by researchers external to the agency is that, in essence, staff who are indigenous to an agency are more likely to be held *accountable* for the effects of the research on the agency's service provision. When individuals such as university faculty conduct research in a human service agency, their involvement with the agency is usually terminated (either temporarily or permanently) when a given research project that they are conducting has been completed. If the research project did not result in a significant or durable improvement in the functioning of the human service agency, there is really no means of evoking the (external) researchers' assistance in continuing to attempt to improve the situation. Actually, the researchers may not even be aware that whatever benefit may have resulted from their research efforts disappeared once the research was over and they had left the agency. In contrast, if the research is conducted by agency staff, there are a number of factors, albeit at times somewhat subtle, that tend to force the staff to continue efforts to make improvements. For one thing, the latter staff continue working within the agency after the research has been completed and they are continuously faced with the existence of the problem that the research was intended to resolve. The continued existence of the problematic situation serves to prompt the agency staff researchers to take additional actions to make the situation better. Relatedly, the scenario can arise in which agency staff who were not involved in the research are aware that a research project was completed but that the research outcome did not significantly impact the agency in a beneficial manner. For example, the research project may have shown good behavior change data, but the data actually represented only a very small part of the situation in the agency that was being addressed. Similarly, the effects of the research project may have lasted only as long as the formal research undertaking lasted. In such situations, the staff who were not involved in the research frequently will let the agency researchers know that the research did not really fulfill its intended purpose, which can further prompt the agency researchers to continue to work on the task that was originally addressed in the research.

By better fulfilling the applied function of applied behavior analysis through the active involvement of human service personnel in research, a growing concern within the professional discipline of behavior analysis can be addressed. That is, it is becoming well recognized that the advancements in technologies for therapeutically changing human behavior that have been reflected in the professional research literature are not being so reflected in the day-to-day practices within existing human service agencies (Christian, 1983). The fact that state-of-the-art therapy strategies exist for the most part only in the rather short-lived demonstration projects of applied researchers (and the journal articles that describe those projects) in many ways attests to the problems inherent in researchers conducting research in human service settings who are not integrally involved in the working operations of those settings. A case will be made in the following chapters that by involving agency staff in applied research within their agency, a much greater likelihood exists that the therapeutic advances that result from applied behavioral research will become a part of the standard operating procedures of human service agencies. Consequently, the gap between the therapeutic knowledge reflected in the professional research literature and that represented in routine operations in applied settings will be reduced significantly.

A final advantage of the approach to applied behavioral research proposed here is basically a benefit for the staff of a human service agency who conduct the research. Specifically, the successful involvement of human service personnel in applied research can significantly enrich the professional development of those staff persons. Participation in good research programs also can make the job of a human service professional considerably more enjoyable. When considered in this light, successful involvement in applied research can help resolve a common and much publicized problem in human service agencies: professional staff burnout. Research involvement can help staff see a useful and permanent outcome to their work efforts, as well as set the occasion for staff to receive commendation and recognition from their professional colleagues. In essence, research activity can add a degree of pleasurable excitement to a staff member's job. Methods of enhancing staff enjoyment through involvement in applied research programs will be discussed in Chapter 6. Further, and probably of more relevance from the point of view of an agency's service provision to its clients, conducting applied behavioral research can often assist a professional staff person in better fulfilling certain components of his/her job responsibilities. As will be discussed in subsequent chapters, the systematic data-based approach to resolving important problem areas within a human service agency that forms the basis of good applied research methodology often results in more significant and longer-lasting resolutions to problem areas than what usually occurs in human service operations. Depending in large part on the nature of an applied researcher's role within a human service agency (Chap. 3), applied behavioral research can make substantial improvements in both *staff performance* by making staff work activities the focus of research and *client welfare* by focusing research efforts directly on client services.

The notion that human service staff should conduct research in their own agency is not particularly novel. Certainly individuals working in human service settings have contributed to the development and growth of applied behavior analysis through conducting and publishing sound research. However, such contributions are quite rare relative to the applied research conducted through the university system. For example, a review of research articles published in the journal that generally is best known for publishing applied behavior analysis research, the *Journal of Applied Behavior Analysis,* indicates that the vast majority — some 80 percent — of the affiliations listed for the authors of those articles are university settings. Nevertheless, the finding that at least *some* of the articles have been published by practitioners in human service agencies indicates that indeed research can be successfully conducted by agency personnel within their own agency.

Purpose of Text

The purpose of this text is to discuss *how* staff in human service agencies can successfully conduct applied behavioral research within their agencies. In contrast to other texts that describe how to do research in terms of the *technical* aspects of experimentation (e.g. how to do statistical analyses, how to establish valid experimental designs, how to select representative sample populations of experimental participants), this text focuses on the *practical* aspects of developing and maintaining a successful research program within the confines of a human service setting. Topics to be discussed include how to synthesize research activities into existing job routines in order to make the research work load manageable and to ensure that agency service responsibilities are not jeopardized (Chap. 2), how to work with different staff within the agency in order to disperse the work load required by good research as well as to share the benefits of doing research (Chap. 3), how to obtain supervisory/administrative support for conducting research as well as how to take advantage of support sources that are external to the agency (Chap. 4), how to select research questions and experimental methodologies that are most amenable to research endeavors in applied settings in order to make research as easy and timely as possible (Chap. 5), how to maintain a productive research program over extended periods of time given the day-by-day working constraints of a human service setting (Chap. 6), and how to facilitate the dissemination and publication aspects of research conducted in a human service agency (Chap. 7).

The strategies to be discussed throughout this text for conducting research while working within a human service agency are based upon procedures that have been previously successful in this type of endeavor. In this regard, *successful* research is defined here as investigations conducted by practitioners working within human service agencies that are published in professional, refereed journals (i.e. journals that require a professional review and determination of the merits of a paper prior to determining whether the paper should be published). Although the criterion of a *published* paper is a rather stringent guideline with which to evaluate the success of research projects (and certainly a view that is not shared among all applied researchers), it is and should be a necessary component of a useful research undertaking in human service settings. The rationale for the importance placed on publishing the results of a research project is basically straightforward: the purpose of applied research in the human services is to acquire information that can advance society's ability to help people in need (as well as to assist the agency in which the research is conducted to improve its services), and that information is of essentially no value to society unless people who can make use of the information have relatively easy access to it. Publication of the information is the best way to provide the necessary access for the most people. Further, by publishing the results of applied research in professional journals, the information becomes a piece of history in terms of a *permanent* product to which people can have continued access.

As just noted, the publication criterion used here for the success of a research project is not a unanimously agreed upon criterion. A somewhat conflicting view regarding the importance (or lack thereof) of publication is that any research can be useful because it forces a human service agency to carefully evaluate, and subsequently improve, its services whether or not the research results in a published product. Indeed, applied behavioral research usually does involve a focus on systematic, data-based strategies that can foster improvements in many human service agencies beyond typical (non-research) problem-solving approaches. However, research is by no means a necessary condition for improving human service delivery; service settings *can* objectively scrutinize their services without requiring the extra time and effort necessary for including publishable research as part of the process. In essence, if research is viewed only as a means of improving an agency's service provision and the publication component is not considered integral in the success of the research, then the personnel conducting the research are likely to be wasting considerable time and energy. The extra time investment necessary to make the improvement process a research undertaking results in no additional benefit to anyone if the research outcome is not published in order to allow access for other persons in the helping professions.

In addition to the primary purpose of sharing relevant information with other professionals, conducting successful (i.e. publishable) research has an *educational value* for staff in human service agencies. A number of applied research journals have a thorough review process for papers that are submitted to the respective journals for publication consideration, and the results of that process are shared with the submitting author. The information obtained through the review process can be extremely educational for the author, especially for new researchers. A good illustration of how an editorial review process can function in an educative manner is represented by the process used by the *Journal of Applied Behavior Analysis* (JABA). When a research paper is submitted to JABA, the paper is assigned by the Editor to an Associate Editor who has established research expertise in the topic addressed by the paper. The Associate Editor then forwards the paper to be reviewed by several members of the editorial board who also have expertise in the area addressed by the research. Additionally, one or more individuals who are not on the journal's editorial board but have relevant experiences pertaining to one or more aspects of the research are usually asked to critique the paper as a Guest Reviewer. What results is three to five independent reviews of the research, plus the Associate Editor's own review. When considering that the comments about the research are coming from some of the (if not *the*) national leaders in the topic area addressed by the research, the value of the information pertaining to a given study is somewhat staggering. It is not uncommon for an author who submits a paper to JABA to receive critiques that encompass some 10-15 pages of typed information across all reviewers.

An example of the outcome of a JABA editorial review is presented in Appendix A. Appendix A provides the editorial correspondence sent to the senior author (in this case, the author of the current text) of a paper submitted to, and eventually published in, JABA (Reid & Hurlbut, 1977). The editorial package includes the editorial letter to the submitting author and four sets of reviewer comments. This particular editorial review was selected to present in the Appendix, because it proved to be quite helpful to the senior author of the paper in terms of improving the submitted manuscript as well as subsequent research undertakings. In addition, this review represents a good model of a competent and thorough review process. Specifically, the reviewer critiques provide a number of positive comments regarding the authors' research, which can be very helpful in encouraging applied researchers to continue their research efforts. Also, a rather large number of detailed suggestions are presented for improving the manuscript as well as for potential related research that could be conducted. The most helpful suggestions in this regard are the similar comments provided by different reviewers about the same aspect of the paper (see also the summary provided in the Associate Editor's letter). When different members of an editorial review board highlight the same part of a manuscript as being problematic, the author of the paper should be clearly convinced that there is a problem with that particular manuscript section.

The information obtained from editorial review processes such as the one used by JABA can be especially helpful in assisting a researcher in improving his/her *future* research endeavors as just noted. For example, a group of practitioner-researchers at Northern Indiana State Hospital and Developmental Disabilities Center once submitted a paper to JABA that demonstrated a method for therapeutically involving institutional staff in sign language training programs with severely handicapped residents (Faw, et al., 1981). An issue raised repeatedly in the reviewer comments as part of the review process was that, although the project was successful in *teaching* the residents how to use manual signing, it was not totally successful, in that the residents did not actually *use* the signing skills during the course of their routine day for communication purposes. Such information was very valuable in the development of a subsequent research project that specifically focused on how to assist severely handicapped persons in an institution in using their signing skills to actually communicate (Schepis et al., 1982).

In completing a successful research endeavor in a human service setting, a number of experimental criteria must be met, ranging from the selection of a socially important topic of research to the use of a valid experimental design. These features of good applied research, although not the main focus of this text from a technical point of view, will be highlighted periodically in regard to practical strategies for incorporating the features into routine operations of a human service agency. In this regard, there is one criterion that is more important than all others in determining the success of an applied investigation: the research project must result in significant changes in the dependent entities (i.e. target behaviors) that the project addresses. Regardless of how well a project is designed and conducted, if it does not bring about substantial changes in whatever aspect of an agency's service provision is focused on during an investigation, then the research will not be successful. On the other hand, sometimes a project that may have some technical flaws in its procedural design or implementation can still be successful if it resulted in significant behavior change. As will be discussed in Chapter 2, this primary characteristic of successful research means that, in essence, if an applied research project conducted in a human service agency is going to be published, it *must* significantly improve a problematic situation within the agency.

Using the basic criteria of successful research as just described, examples of a variety of research projects will be referenced in the following chapters in light of day-to-day activities that went into the research projects and were instrumental in the eventual success of the investigations. Again, the activities to be described will not be of a *technical* nature, but instead, of a practical concern, such as, for example, how to conduct research when one already has a full-time clinical or administrative job, how to obtain assistance to conduct all of the necessary work that goes into a research project when nobody in the agency has any background in research, and how to overcome negative perceptions of (and responses to) research that are often held by staff working in human service agencies.

Basic Premises For Conducting Research Within Applied Settings

In order to conduct successful applied research in human service settings, there are two basic premises that must be adhered to. These premises will be referred to repeatedly throughout the text, because without them, the chances of initiating and maintaining a productive research program in a human service agency are virtually nonexistent. The first premise is that all staff who conduct research in a human service agency must keep *the service mission of the agency as their first priority.* Specifically, client services must always be the primary concern for all agency staff, and those services should never be sacrificed for research or any other reason. Hence, it is incumbent upon the individual who wants to conduct research to do so in close conjunction with the ongoing agency mission of providing services to clients. The rationale for this premise is that a human service agency's main purpose for existence is to provide services to people in need, and anyone who works for the agency, including a researcher, is employed to fulfill that purpose. Otherwise, if an agency staff member has as a first priority the conducting of research, the same obstacles that face researchers who are external to a given agency such as university faculty who attempt to do research in the agency as discussed earlier will arise, in that the mission of the agency staff member/researcher will be at odds with the mission of the agency.

The second premise for conducting applied behavioral research in human service agencies is that if an agency staff member is interested in conducting and disseminating research, he/she *must be willing to work diligently*. In short, doing good research requires a very considerable amount of hard work. Although this text will describe various means of reducing the work load involved in research, there nevertheless will continue to be a significant amount of effort required of an agency staff person who wants to conduct successful research. If a practitioner is not willing to work at least periodically at intensities that are above and beyond the level that the typical staff member in a human service agency works, then he/she should give up any thoughts of being successful at conducting good applied research.

The importance of an individual being willing to work quite diligently in order to develop a successful research program cannot be over-emphasized. Unfortunately, however, in many human service agencies there is rather subtle discouragement against diligent work habits. In typical human service settings, for example, it is generally assumed that staff are held more accountable for their work time than are faculty in academic settings. To illustrate, records for time worked such as mechanized time cards and time clocks, sign-in and sign-out sheets, etc., often are commonplace for professionals in human service agencies but not for faculty in universities. One paradoxical result of such accountability systems is that human service staff become accustomed to viewing their workday on a scheduled, fixed-hour basis (e.g. eight-to-five). To successfully conduct research while being employed in a human service agency, a staff member cannot be restricted to a fixed schedule or a fixed amount of work time. Rather, he/she must be willing to work at least intermittently, however many hours during the day or week that are necessary, to ensure that a given component of a research project is completed satisfactorily. Relatedly, a staff member who desires to be a productive researcher cannot be overly concerned as to whether he/she receives official work-time credit for the hours worked on a research project. The extra hours worked should not be restricted to regulations in regard to earning compensatory time or overtime; the hours should be worked (even if on the staff member's own time) in regard to whatever amount of time is necessary to conduct the research. Of course, willingness to work extra hours regardless of whether the time is considered approved time for pay or not is one of the trademarks of a true professional in a human service agency, regardless of involvement in research. This is not to say that a staff member must be a workaholic to be a successful researcher, only that he/she must be willing to periodically work more hours than the usual human service employee.

Personnel Who Can Conduct Research in Human Service Settings

Although this text does not, for the most part, discuss the technical aspects of research, such aspects are nevertheless vital to conducting good research. Consequently, there are limits as to the audience for whom this text will be of benefit. The book is primarily intended for those persons working in human service settings, or considering working in such, who already have a basic knowledge of the technicalities of research, perferably through training and experience in applied behavior analysis and/ or behavior modification. However, this does not mean that the intended audience is only skilled researchers; it means that those readers who will most benefit from the text are persons who already have a pretty good knowledge base about the basics of research, although they might not be experienced in conducting and publishing applied research. Further, the text is directed to readers who *want* to do research but perhaps are having difficulty in conducting and publishing research due to the constraints of working in a non-research-oriented service setting. For the sake of clarity and consistency, the type of person to whom this text is primarily intended (i.e. the reader who has a basic knowledge of research techniques and wants to do research) will be referred to as a *senior researcher* throughout the text. Most frequently, the senior researcher will be the individual in a human service agency who has the most training and/or experience in applied behavior analysis. The senior researcher may be, for example, a school psychologist with master's-level training in behavior analysis, a Ph.D. psychologist within an institution for the mentally retarded with hands-on experience with behavior modification, an educational administrator who has acquired research knowledge through work with university faculty or students, or a bachelor's trained clinician who has acquired knowledge in behavior analysis through his/her own initiative and reading. As a point of reference for the reader, the author of this text functions as a senior researcher (as the term is used here) and administrator in a human service setting.

The use of the term *senior researcher* to refer to the role described in this text is somewhat different than how the term has been traditionally used. Generally, a *senior* researcher is used to refer to someone who is well recognized for having published numerous research articles. Again, as used here, the term refers to an individual employed in a human service setting who has basic knowledge in research technology—more so than the typical human service practitioner—whether or not the individual has ever conducted research.

A secondary target for this text is agency staff members, particularly upper-level executives and administrators, who desire to develop and/or expand a research program within their agency by employing and working with, or supervising, a senior researcher-type individual. In the latter case, this text is intended to help the agency executive know what to expect (and/or manage) of an applied researcher in order to have a successful and enjoyable research program in his/her human service agency.

REFERENCES

Baer, D. M., Wolf, M. M., & Risley, T. R. (1968). Some current dimensions of applied behavior analysis. *Journal of Applied Behavior Analysis, 1,* 91-97.

Christian, W. P. (1983). A case study in programming and maintenance of institutional change. *Journal of Organizational Behavior Management, 3/4,* 99-153.

Faw, G. D., Reid, D. H., Schepis, M. M., Fitzgerald, J. R., & Welty, P. A. (1981). Involving institutional staff in the development and maintenance of sign language skills with profoundly retarded persons. *Journal of Applied Behavior Analysis, 14,* 411-423.

Liberman, R. P. (1983). Guest editor's preface. *Analysis and Intervention in Developmental Disabilities, 2/3,* iii.

Reid, D. H. & Hurlbut, B. (1977). Teaching nonvocal communication skills to multihandicapped retarded adults. *Journal of Applied Behavior Analysis, 10,* 591-603.

Schepis, M. M., Reid, D. H., Fitzgerald, J. R., Faw, G. D., van den Pol, R. A., & Welty, P. A. (1982). A program for increasing manual signing by autistic and profoundly retarded youth within the daily environment. *Journal of Applied Behavior Analysis, 15,* 363-379.

Chapter 2

SYNTHESIZING RESEARCH INTO THE DAILY JOB RESPONSIBILITIES OF A HUMAN SERVICE PRACTITIONER

CONDUCTING and publishing research is an activity that many professionals employed in human service settings would welcome. Indeed, many practitioners and administrators have expressed a rather serious desire to be involved in applied research, or at least have someone under their supervision conduct research. However, such expressions of interest in research are almost always accompanied by the qualification that it is not possible to conduct research given the time- and effort-consuming service responsibilities required of personnel in most human service agencies. The daily administrative, supervisory and/or clinical duties seem to encompass all of an individual's work time, thereby prohibiting time for research. Undoubtedly, daily job responsibilities *are* very time consuming as they should be; fulfilling service obligations is exactly why a staff member is employed by an agency. Consequently, the only way to really develop a successful research program in human service settings is to *synthesize research activities into daily job responsibilities* such that both types of activities can occur simultaneously.

The purpose of this chapter is to discuss *how* research activities can be synthesized into the ongoing work duties of a senior researcher (as the term was defined in Chapter 1) in a human service agency. The basic premise of the chapter is that if an applied investigation is conducted such that a research finding of (publishable) interest occurs *and* job responsibilities are simultaneously fulfilled, then the problem of finding time for research beyond the time required by the daily work routine is greatly reduced or eliminated. Hence, the task is to design research projects that explicitly improve an agency's service provision (albeit even if

17

only on a small scale) while at the same time answering an important experimental question that will make a contribution to the research literature and a professional discipline.

Selecting a Research Topic That Improves an Agency's Service Provision

As just alluded to, the first step in synthesizing applied research into the ongoing work routine in a human service setting is to choose a research project that assists in fulfilling a given job responsibility. One particularly helpful means of selecting an appropriate research topic in this regard is to maintain a list of problems within one's job domain that need to be resolved. Subsequently, a research project can be selected that will evaluate a method of resolving one of the problems on the problem list. When considered in this light, the most appropriate type of research to conduct in human services settings is *applied, problem-solving research.* That is, a senior researcher should be an *applied* researcher. The main point is that if an experimentally substantiated means of resolving a given problem in a human service agency can be documented, then valuable information will be generated through the successful resolution of the problem that should be disseminated (i.e. through the applied research literature) to other human service professionals such that they can use the information to solve similar types of problems.

By maintaining a list of problems within a respective job situation, there is usually no dearth of possible topics for applied research. If an individual is employed as a clinician, for example, there is undoubtedly a number of difficult and/or unique training or therapy problems that arise across clients. Finding successful resolutions to the therapy problems represents a means of establishing an applied research project. Client-related clinical problems that have been resolved through previous applied research projects in human service settings have been numerous and varied, ranging from how to reduce dangerous self-injurious behavior of mentally retarded clients (Dorsey, et al., 1982) to how to improve student attentiveness in school classrooms (Hooper & Reid, 1985). Relatedly, there are frequently obstacles encountered by clinicians when attempting to evoke caregiver assistance in proficiently implementing client treatment regimes that could represent the focus of applied research projects. To illustrate, enlisting the assistance of direct care staff in carrying out therapeutic types of interactions with institutionalized clients has been a widespread problem in residential facilities for the mentally retarded. Consequently, a number of applied problem-solving investigations have focused on developing methods of improving therapeutic staff-resident interactions (e.g. Burg, Reid & Lattimore, 1979; Burgio, Whitman, & Reid, 1983; Montegar et al., 1977). Similarly, from the point of view of an administrator or supervisor, it is quite likely that problems with staff performance arise from time to time (or as in some cases, never really go away) that could be addressed within an agency from an applied research standpoint. Examples of the latter types of problems that have been addressed through problem-solving research conducted by human service personnel include staff absenteeism (Shoemaker & Reid, 1980), infrequent intra-agency staff communication (Quilitch, 1978), ineffective implementation of client training programs (Kissle, Whitman & Reid, 1982), and inadequate administrative record-keeping performance (Repp & Deitz, 1979).

In generating a problem list as an impetus for initiating research, it is usually quite helpful, if not essential, for a senior researcher to involve his/her colleagues, supervisors and/or supervisees in the process. The rationale for such involvement is several-fold. For one thing, as will be discussed in depth in Chapter 3, the type of problem-solving research discussed here can almost never be accomplished in human service settings by one person single-handedly; there is simply too much work to be done. Hence, a senior researcher must collaborate with other agency staff members in order to conduct research. When people do collaborate on a research topic, then their collaboration is usually more productive if they are involved in initially determining the specific problem to investigate. In particular, if the focus of a research project is an agency problem that a colleague of a senior researcher identifies, then it is more likely that the colleague will be seriously interested in resolving the problem (and, consequently, more interested in carrying out the research responsibilities) than if the identified problem was only the senior researcher's idea. In regard to involving a senior researcher's *supervisees* in the selection of a research topic, in many cases the likelihood of selecting a truly relevant problem to resolve is also enhanced. More specifically, in most cases the staff whom a professional such as a senior researcher in a human service agency supervises are usually more intimately aware of the "front-line" problems that any agency faces on a day-to-day basis, because they have more contact with those problems than persons higher up in the organizational hierarchy. In human service agencies, the "front-line" problems usually refer to issues involving direct service delivery to clients. Problematic areas pertaining to direct client services should be a priority for agency problem solving and, hence, for applied, problem-solving research.

An example of how the process just noted can be employed to select research topics that address agency problems is reflected in a line of research conducted in schools serving severely handicapped persons. Marsha Parsons, a school principal, began generating a list of problems and subsequently identified her most serious issue as *what* her education staff were teaching their severely handicapped students. Being responsible for the overall school program, Marsha had serious concern over whether what was being taught to her students was really of any significant benefit to the students once they left the school classrooms; it was not evident that the student skills targeted by the teachers would assist the students to function in their routine living, work or recreational environments. This concern of Marsha's (that was specifically identified in the process of generating a problem list) subsequently resulted in a program of research designed to: (a) develop and validate a more purposeful teaching curriculum for severely handicapped students (Reid, et al., 1985) and (b) develop and demonstrate a wide-scale staff training and supervision approach for assisting educators in implementing the curriculum (Parsons et al., 1987). The research projects that had their beginning in the problem list developed by the school principal eventually impacted four school programs and over 150 severely handicapped persons in terms of their involvement in a more appropriate educational program.

Conducting a sequence of investigations as just noted to solve related service-delivery problems can result in a very significant improvement in an agency's service provision as well as result in several contributions to the professional research literature. However, such a sequential, multi-experiment approach to applied research usually requires several years for completion and considerable patience on the part of the researchers. Relatedly, this type of long-term undertaking is usually best accomplished when the researchers and/or supervisory personnel remain constant within a human service agency for the multi-year duration of the research program. Unfortunately, long-term consistency of professional personnel within a given human service agency is not always possible. As a result, many research projects that begin on a sound basis do not eventually succeed because a key member of the research team resigns from the human service agency and his/her former research responsibilties are not assumed by someone else due to lack of ability and/or interest. An alternative and generally more expedient means of conducting applied research than implementig a series of related investigations is to focus on rather singular problem areas. That is, in contrast to resolving a problem area that requires a sequence of time- and effort-consuming interventions (i.e. several applied investigations), an area that is more circumscribed in nature can be targeted. (See Chapter 6 for a discussion of the relative advantages and disadvantages of conducting independent research projects versus developing a long-term program of research.) In the latter situations, a specific problem is selected from the problem list for resolution through *one* applied research investigation. For example, two administrators, Chris Schuh and Dora Brannon, were interested in resolving the problem of excessive absenteeism among direct care staff in a residential facility for developmentally disabled persons. Consequently, an applied research study was conducted to develop and experimentally evaluate a means of reducing absenteeism (Reid, Schuh-Wear, & Brannon, 1978). The study served the service purpose for the agency of reducing staff absenteeism *and* the research purpose of demonstrating for other agencies how to reduce staff absences. Similarly, another administrator, Judy Shoemaker, focused on the rather circumscribed problem of infrequent parental contact with severely handicapped residents of a state residential facility by demonstrating through an applied study how to increase parent involvement with their institutionalized children (Shoemaker & Reid, 1980). On a more direct client-service level, Ann Lagomarcino used a problem-solving research approach in her role as Director of Therapeutic Recreation in a state institution to improve the leisure skills and recreational opportunities of severely and profoundly mentally retarded persons. Ann's specific goal was to develop and experimentally evaluate a training program for teaching dance skills to her clients such that they could better participate in community dance activites — a goal that was successfully achieved (Lagomarcino, et al., 1984).

Throughout the remainder of this text, research will be referred to in light of the problem-solving format just described and exemplified in the studies just cited. It is strongly contended that this type of applied research is the most important kind of research to conduct in human service agencies, because it serves the dual purpose of improving a given agency's service provision and advancing the human service profession in general. It is also strongly contended that basic experimentation *should not* be conducted in non-university-based human service agencies. The latter contention is by no means universally agreed upon by researchers, professionals or academicians in the human services. Nevertheless, there are a number of reasons for asserting that basic experimentation has no place in typical human service settings. First, frequently human service agencies are relatively understaffed in terms of fulfilling their client service responsibilities in a highly proficient manner; to draw away skilled staff resources from an already understaffed agency in order to work on (basic) research that will have no bearing on the agency's services to its clients is, at best, somewhat unprofessional, and at worse, unethical. Second, university programs usually are far better equipped with resources to do basic research than typical human service agencies and have the designated mission of conducting such research. Hence, the most appropriate site for basic experimentation is academic research settings, not applied settings. Third, based on the author's experience as well as that of other practitioners, the history of basic research in human service settings has generally been rather dismal in terms of the impact it leaves on staff members who make their living by working in human service agencies. Attempts to conduct non-problem-solving research in many human service settings have left practitioners with a negative impression of the role of research and have caused serious resistance among agency staff to subsequent attempts to conduct research in those settings, even if the subsequent research plans are problem solving in nature. Some of the problems associated with basic research undertakings in human service agencies are elaborated on in Chapter 3.

The problems with basic research as just summarized in regard to investigations conducted in human service settings should not be interpreted as a devaluation of this type of research. Much of what has developed from basic research laboratories has been crucial in eventually leading to highly significant improvements in many aspects of the helping professions and, of particular concern here, to the development of applied behavior analysis. The main point is not that basic research should not occur but that it should not occur in typical human service settings. In short, senior researchers interested in conducting basic experimentation should seek employment in academically related research institutions, not in human service agencies. The latter should be the site for senior researchers interested in conducting only applied, problem-solving research.

Selecting a Topic That Will Contribute to the Professional Field

Once a research question is selected that focuses on resolving a problematic situation within a human service agency, then a second criterion becomes crucial if indeed the research is to be successful: the research question must be one that, when answered experimentally, will make a contribution to the human service field or some component thereof. Generally, resolution of the applied problem that is to be addressed through a research project within a human service agency will make a contribution to the professional field if: (a) the problem is encountered by other agencies such that other practitioners could benefit from becoming aware of a successful means of resolving the problem and (b) methods and demonstrations of successfully resolving the problem are not currently readily apparent in the professional literature. In regard to the latter point, there are numerous variations of human service problems and methods of resolving those problems that can be addressed in a given research project to enhance the project's potential contribution to the field. An awareness of such variations, and in essence, an awareness of what types of research questions will result in contributions to the human service field, requires a rather strong familiarity with existing professional literature.

In typical human service settings, the vast majority of personnel are not familiar with the existing research literature. Consequently, the senior researcher in the agency must assume the responsibility of being (and staying) knowledgeable about relevant professional literature. In actuality, this individual is usually the only person within human service agencies who has the necessary background in terms of technical research knowledge to be able to be very familiar with past and current research literature. Unfortunately (at least from the point of view of conducting good applied research), staying abreast of research developments and current literature can be quite time consuming. Hence, specific strategies are required in order to allow a senior researcher to be able to stay abreast of the applied research literature while simultaneously fulfilling his/her daily job responsibilities. Workable strategies for maintaining familiarity with the professional literature while working in a human service setting are discussed in detail in Chapter 7. For the purpose of discussion here, it is usually safe to assume that if an agency has a serious problem and an applied researcher is not aware of any readily available solutions to that problem, then demonstrating how to resolve the problem through an applied research project will probably represent a contribution to the human service field.

Getting Research Going and Keeping It Going
As Part of the Daily Job Routine

Once a relevant problem and subsequent research question have been selected, the next step in initiating a research program in a human service setting is to design the study. Here again, it is incumbent upon the senior researcher to design essentially all aspects of the investigation, because he/she is usually the only person within a human service agency who is trained in the necessary research skills. It is beyond the purpose of this text to discuss the technical aspects of how to design an applied research study, although some suggestions for selecting experimental designs that most easily fit within the typical operations of human service agencies are provided in Chapter 5.*

When the basic design of an experiment has been determined, it is then the senior researcher's role to actually initiate the study proper in terms of collecting initial data. At this point, the researcher's staff, colleagues and/or supervisor(s) need to become heavily (re)involved in the investigation (i.e. they should have been initially involved in selecting the research topic). As noted earlier, conducting applied research in human service settings requires considerable work; to be successful, *research work must involve more than one researcher.* In subsequent sections of this text (and particularly in Chapter 3), methods for involving agency personnel in addition to the senior researcher in research activities will be discussed.

Before continuing the discussion of how to synthesize research into daily job responsibilities, a word of caution is warranted regarding the role of the senior researcher in working with his/her agency colleagues and/or supervisees on research projects as just referred to. Specifically, an applied researcher needs to guard against becoming *too dependent* on the research co-workers. Because of numerous competing administrative, clinical and/or supervisory responsibilities, once the daily implementation of a research project is being largely conducted by the applied researcher's co-workers on the project, then the senior researcher is likely to spend all his/her time responding to the competing (non-research) responsiblities of the human service agency and not to the ongoing investigation. Such a situation can become problematic, because the staff co-workers often do not have sufficient research expertise to

---

*The interested reader is referred to Bailey & Bostow (1979), Barlow & Hersen (1984), and Kazdin (1982) for relevant discussions in this regard.

appropriately respond to the seemingly endless array of questions that arise during the implementation of an applied research project, including, for example, determining when data collection is becoming too inconsistent due to concellations of observation sessions, determining when a sufficient amount of data and/or stability in the data has occurred in order to change experimental conditions, and so forth. Hence, mistakes in the implementation of the research procedures can occur if a senior researcher is not intimately aware of the ongoing activities, and by the time the senior researcher does become aware of the mistakes, the investigation is already in serious trouble or actually ruined in terms of providing valid data on how to resolve an agency problem. This type of situation in which an applied researcher loses close contact with a research project is somewhat common in human service settings. To avoid this undesirable situation from developing, a senior researcher *must find a way to maintain very frequent contact with the ongoing project,* usually by incorporating some specific research functions into what he/she does on a daily basis as part of the routine job.

Maintaining Frequent Contact With an Ongoing Research Project

There are several strategies that can help a senior researcher maintain contact with an ongoing investigation that is being conducted primarily by co-workers. Perhaps the most advantageous method is to design the data collection part of the investigation, or some component thereof, such that co-workers turn in the raw data following each experimental session to the senior experimenter, who in turn has the responsibility of summarizing and graphing the data. This process has several advantages. First, it provides the senior researcher with a frequent, visible prompt via the data sheets to attend to the ongoing project. For example, co-workers can give the data to a secretary who in turn puts it in a senior researcher's daily incoming mailbox. Subsequently, as daily incoming mail is reviewed by the senior researcher, there is always contact with the research project from which the data came. A second advantage is that, by being responsible for the analysis of the raw data that has to be conducted in order to graph the data, the senior researcher maintains close contact with the performance of the experimental participants in the study as well as the performance of the staff (i.e. observers) who are collecting the data. Of course, such contact is not as valuable for the senior researcher as is direct observation of experimental sessions or procedures as a means of keeping the senior researcher informed about a project; direct observation is usually crucial to ensure appropriate implementation of the experimental methodology. However, direct observation usually requires the senior researcher to be at the specific experimental site at a specified time, and such arrangements are not always possible on a daily (or even weekly) basis given other job responsibilities of the senior researcher. In contrast, time for reviewing and analyzing raw data on data sheets can be more easily scheduled around other routine job responsibilites.

A third advantage of the senior researcher being responsible for the initial data calculations on a research project is that, by maintaining the up-to-date data summaries or graphs, co-workers will often seek out the senior researcher to review the data because of their interst in knowing how the project (and their efforts) is proceeding. The interactions that the staff colleagues on a research project initiate with the senior researcher further prompt the senior researcher to attend to the research project through relevant discussions with the co-workers.

In contrast to the advantages just noted, a disadvantage of the senior researcher being responsible for keeping the data analysis up-to-date on an ongoing investigation is that the process can become excessively time consuming for the senior researcher. Also, in one sense it is not a very logical process when considering maximum use of available resources. That is, other agency personnel usually have, or can acquire relatively easily, the skills necessary to perform various data calculations and graphing that the senior researcher is doing, whereas only the senior researcher may possess the skills to perform other components of a research project. An alternative method of structuring frequent contact between the senior researcher and an ongoing research project is for the researcher to always schedule at least a few minutes per day attending to some aspect of the project as part of his/her daily work routine. To illustrate, such attention could be added to the daily and weekly "to-do" lists of the senior researcher, along with various non-research job tasks. The attention may take the form of observing an experimental session, conversing with a staff person who is assisting with the project, and/or merely *thinking* about how a particular investigation is progressing and what could be changed to improve the study. Providing frequent attention to ongoing research projects in this manner often not only helps a senior researcher maintain awareness of how a research project is proceeding, it also can serve to enhance the senior researcher's *non-research* job performance.

Being involved in applied research activities frequently can serve to prompt a senior researcher to become more directly aware of day-to-day agency operations that he/she should be aware of as part of the routine job role. For example, a rather frequent complaint among staff in human service settings such as residential facilities and schools for mentally retarded or psychiatric populations is that professionals (e.g. psychologists, senior administrators) rarely spend time where the service is actually being provided to clients such as an institutional ward or classroom in contrast to spending time in the professionals' offices or meeting rooms. Consequently, many professionals are not very aware of what is taking place in regard to direct service provision. The interest that research generates in terms of the senior researcher wanting to directly see how things are proceeding with a research project frequently can prompt him/her to leave the office and come into direct contact with staff and clients in a wide variety of work environments. Such contact helps the senior researcher to be more directly aware of how well various agency responsibilities are being fulfilled while at the same time allowing the researcher to stay abreast of the ongoing research activities. The contact within different agency work sites also makes the senior researcher more visible to agency staff—an outcome that can significantly enhance a senior researcher's rapport with agency staff and, subsequently, the ability to establish a successful applied research program in a human service setting. (See Chapter 3 for elaboration on the importance of an applied researcher's rapport with staff.)

Being Willing and Able to Engage in All Aspects of Research

In considering the involvement of an agency's senior researcher in performing various aspects of a research project as part of the daily job routine, including involvement in the initial data summary as just discussed, a concern that often arises is whether an advanced graduate-level-trained individual (e.g. a Ph.D.) such as a senior researcher should *ever* have to engage in these types of seemingly low-skilled tasks. A common view among professionals is that they did not spend years of effort and expense in graduate school simply to later spend their time in clerical-type tasks. Indeed, for the reason of maximization of available staff resources for conducting research as noted earlier, there may be some merit to this view. However, all things considered, there is actually *very little* merit in this line of reasoning. If a senior researcher is to be truly successful in conducting research in human service settings, he/she must be *able and willing to engage in all aspects of research activities* on an as-needed basis.

There are several reasons for asserting that senior researchers must be ready to participate in any and all aspects of conducting a research project. First, because the vast majority of personnel in applied settings do not know how to conduct research, the senior researcher usually has to teach a variety of research skills to certain agency staff in order to be able to conduct research. Probably the most effective way to teach staff is to first *show* staff how to perform various procedures, and the only way to show staff is for the senior researcher to enter the designated work environment and perform the appropriate tasks. Second, by actually conducting various research procedures—be it functioning as an observer, client trainer, data calculator or whatever—the senior researcher can gain a little respect among agency staff persons. In this regard, a common criticism of many highly trained researchers in applied settings is that they tend to consider themselves as "white knights on white horses" and prefer not to get involved in the day-to-day job duties that other agency staff do routinely. When staff view a senior researcher in such a light, they are not likely to be very receptive to working with the researcher on a given research project. Further, staff who have this impression of an applied researcher are likely to make the researcher's task rather unpleasant and/or difficult to perform. To illustrate, staff dislike for a senior reseacher, because of the latter's "holier-than-thou" attitude, can result in staff complaining about a research project to other staff persons and generating resistance to the research activities. Actually, staff can essentially destroy a research project through various means, including complaining to an agency's upper administration to stop a given research project, carrying out experimental procedures inappropriately, and getting participating clients (i.e. experimental subjects) transferred to other program areas within the agency in order to remove them from an ongoing research project. Although these types of resistive activities are rather extreme examples of staff negativism toward research and researchers, they do occur periodically, and a likely impetus to initiate this type of reaction is for a senior researcher to carry a "white knight" type of attitude. In many cases, the most effective way for a senior researcher to prevent and/or overcome such resistance on the part of agency staff members is to actually demonstrate that he/she is able and willing to do whatever needs to be done—and to *repeatedly* demonstrate such skills and willingness whenever and wherever needed.

An additional reason exists for a senior researcher to be willing to engage in all implementation aspects of an ongoing study that relates to the likely success of the project. It is of rather paramount importance for an applied researcher to be successful in his/her first research undertakings in a given human service agency. The chances of success in this regard are enhanced if the senior researcher is very actively involved in the research project. In essence, because the senior researcher is the agency staff person with the most training in research procedures, he/she should be the person who can actually carry out the research procedures most competently. Hence, the more work on the research project that the senior researcher performs, the more likely it is that procedures will be conducted proficiently and, subsequently, the more likely it is that the project will succeed.

There are two main reasons why it is of critical importance that the initial research undertakings of a senior researcher in a human service agency be successful. First, if the research is successful, collaborating staff members, as well as other agency staff persons, will be able to observe the benefits of research in terms of an agency problem being resolved and a contribution being made to the human service field (e.g. a journal article). As a result, agency staff are likely to become more appreciative of applied behavioral research and be more supportive of subsequent research activities of the senior researcher. In contrast, if the research is not successful, in that it does not resolve the problematic situation within the agency that was addressed by the research and no contribution is made to the professional field, there will be essentially no rewards for staff who collaborated on the research project. In the latter case, the senior researcher will probably have a more difficult time evoking staff assistance on research projects in the future and will continue to have difficulty obtaining assistance until some success is achieved with research activities.

The second reason that it is important to be successful with initial research projects is that the *senior researcher him/herself* needs to be rewarded for the considerable effort that generally is required to complete a research project. Applied researchers, especially new researchers, can become discouraged relatively easily when their first attempts to conduct research result in failures. Hence, again, it is beneficial for a senior researcher to spend as much time actually conducting the procedural components of an initial research project along with staff collaborators to maximize the probability of success on the project.

Avoiding Inconsistency in Implementation of Experimental Procedures

In addition to the reasons just noted regarding why a senior researcher must be able and willing to conduct any procedural part of an investigation, a reason exists that pertains to one of the most serious obstacles to conducting research in applied settings: inconsistency in carrying out experimental procedures due to staff researchers being drawn away from research activities into other job responsibilities. Invariably, individuals who are performing a vital function within an ongoing research project will have to intermittently discontinue their involvement at least temporarily because of unanticipated increases in other job-related demands. Such interruptions can cause nightmares for the applied researcher in terms of the threat of destruction of an ongoing investigation. However, all things must be kept in perspective and, again, fulfilling service responsibilities within an agency is the top job priority for all staff, including researchers. Consequently, a senior researcher should assume from the onset of a research project that there will be times when his/her co-workers must be drawn away from an ongoing project. It is most productive, therefore, to actually *plan* before a research project is initiated how to cover temporary staff absences from the research project. One useful approach is for the senior researcher to fill in during temporary staff absences and to conduct the necessary procedures until staff can resume their research duties; hence, the senior researcher must be able and willing to perform whatever aspect of the research project that needs to be accomplished in a given colleague's absence.

One of the most useful areas for a senior researcher to cover during temporary absence of his/her research co-workers is in collecting observational data. Typically, research using an applied behavior analysis paradigm requires a very considerable amount of observational data in terms of measuring the dependent variable (and to a lesser degree, the independent variable). Due in part to the large amount of data that must be collected in a research project, as well as the high frequency with which it must be collected, data collection is an aspect of applied research implementation that often becomes inconsistent or inadvertently discontinued in investigations in human service settings due to temporary absences of research staff. If the senior researcher can fill in during temporary absences of observers and collect reliable data, research projects are much more likely to run smoothly. Actually, in most situations, data collection is relatively easy for the senior researcher to help with, because he/she is usually the person who initially developed the observation system (see comments in the first part of this section) and, consequently, the senior researcher should be quite familiar with the observational process.

Other aspects of conducting research often are more difficult for a senior researcher to assist with during temporary staff absences than collecting observational data. In particular, if the research project involves direct client intervention (e.g. teaching a handicapped client new skills, conducting a behavior deceleration project with an aggressive client), frequently a new person—new in terms of interacting with the client(s)—such as the senior researcher cannot fill in very easily for a staff person who has routinely carried out the client intervention part of the research. In such cases, the senior researcher is not likely to have sufficient rapport with the client due to not having worked with the client. Similarly, the senior researcher is not always motorically proficient in carrying out certain client intervention procedures due to not having practiced the procedures for some time. To avoid these types of situations from arising in which it would be difficult, or even counterproductive, to temporarily replace a research co-worker, plans should be initiated where possible at the onset of a research project to systematically involve several staff persons in the intervention phase of a project such that they can fill in for each other when needed. To illustrate, in a research project designed to evaluate the relative merits of involving profoundly mentally retarded persons in family-style meal processes in contrast to traditional, institutional meals, Phil Wilson in his role as staff psychologist and research co-worker trained several institutional staff members in the behavior change intervention used to teach the family-style dining skills to the clients (Wilson et al., 1984). When one co-worker who routinely conducted the intervention was unavailable in Phil's project, another co-worker who was already familiar with the clients (and vice versa) as well as the intervention process was able to fill in immediately during the staff absence and thereby avoid a disruption in the investigation.

An alternative method that a senior researcher can use to avoid disruptions in an ongoing research project is to help a co-worker complete a *non-research* job responsibility that competes with a research function. That is, when it becomes necessary for a research co-worker who is conducting an important part of a research project to spend more time on another agency work task relative to the research duties, the senior researcher may conduct the non-research work activity for the co-worker such that the co-worker can continue with the research program. For example, during Pam Fabry's work in experimentally evaluating a program to train foster grandparents in methods of teaching severely handicapped clients (Fabry & Reid, 1978), her participation in a rather crucial training session of the research was in potential jeopardy because she needed to attend an habilitative staffing for a client with whom she had worked. The senior researcher (the text author, in this case) could not fill in for Pam in the research activity because he did not know the foster grandparents very well (and vice versa). However, with Pam's briefing, he could fill in for her at the client staffing. Consequently, a disruption in the ongoing research project was avoided because Pam could continue with the research activities and not have to attend the staffing.

Spending a Little Time on Research Every Day

All of the strategies discussed in this chapter section have been effective in past research projects in terms of assisting a senior researcher in initiating a research project and maintaining the project as part of the daily job routine in a human service setting. However, overall, probably the most important strategy in this regard is that *a senior researcher should not let a day go by without spending at least some time working on an ongoing project,* at least while the project is in its initial stages. As noted earlier, there are many ways a senior researcher can spend time on a given project, ranging from observing experimental sessions to thinking about how a project is proceeding. In essence, probably the best indicator of whether a research project will succeed or not is the *frequency* with which a senior researcher works on the project; the more frequently the senior researcher attends to the investigation, the more likely it is that the project will result in a successful outcome. This is not to say that the senior researcher needs to spend several hours a day working on the project; that amount of time would not be possible in many human service agencies due to other responsibilities of the senior researcher within the agency. Actually, if a senior researcher is required to spend several hours a day on one research project on a regular basis, then he/she is probably not managing the involvement of the staff research collaborators very effectively (see Chapter 3 for elaboration). However, a smaller amount of time (often 10-30 minutes) is invariably needed to make sure that a project is running smoothly. To ensure that a research project does indeed succeed, a senior researcher should plan from the beginning of a research project to work on the project at least for a little while every day; if that commitment cannot be made, then the senior researcher should not embark on a given research undertaking.

REFERENCES

Bailey, J. S., & Bostow, D. E. (1979). *Research methods in applied behavior analysis.* Tallahassee, FL: Copy Grafix.

Barlow, D. H., & Hersen, M. (1984). *Single case experimental designs: Strategies for studying behavior change.* New York: Pergamon Press.

Burg, M. M., Reid, D. H., & Lattimore, J. (1979). Use of a self-recording and supervision program to change institutional staff behavior. *Journal of Applied Behavior Analysis, 12,* 363-375.

Burgio, L. D., Whitman, T. L., & Reid, D. H. (1983). A participative management approach for improving direct-care staff performance in an institutional setting. *Journal of Applied Behavior Analysis, 16,* 37-53.

Dorsey, M. F., Iwata, B. A., Reid, D. H., & Davis, P. A. (1982). Protective equipment: Continuous and contingent application in the treatment of self-injurious behavior. *Journal of Applied Behavior Analysis, 15,* 217-230.

Fabry, P. L., & Reid, D. H. (1978). Teaching foster grandparetns to train severely handicapped persons. *Journal of Applied Behavior Analysis, 11,* 111-123.

Hooper, J., & Reid, D. H. (1985). A simple environmental re-design for improving classroom performance of profoundly retarded students. *Education and Treatment of Children, 8,* 25-39.

Kazdin, A. E. (1982). *Single-case research designs: Methods for clinical and applied settings.* New York: Oxford University Press.

Kissel, R. C., Whitman, T. L., & Reid, D. H. (1983). An institutional staff training and self-management program for developing multiple self-care skills in severely/profoundly retarded individuals. *Journal of Applied Behavior Analysis, 16,* 395-415.

Lagomarcino, A., Reid, D. H., Ivancic, M. T., & Faw, G. D. (1984). Leisure-dance instruction for severely and profoundly retarded persons: Teaching an intermediate community-living skill. *Journal of Applied Behavior Analysis, 17,* 71-84.

Montegar, C. A., Reid, D. H., Madsen, C. H., & Ewell, M.D. (1977). Increasing institutional staff-to-resident interactions through in-service training and supervisor approval. *Behavior Therapy, 8,* 533-540.

Parsons, M. B., Schepis, M. M., Reid, D. H., McCarn, J. M., & Green, C. W. (1987). *Expanding the impact of behavioral staff management: A wide-scale, long-term application in schools serving severely handicapped students.* Journal of Applied Behavior Analysis, in press.

Quilitch, H. R. (1978). Using a simple feedback procedure to reinforce the submission of written suggestions by mental health employees. *Journal of Organizational Behavior Management, 1,* 155-163.

Reid, D. H., Parsons, M. B., McCarn, J. M., Green, C. W., Phillips, J. F., & Schepis, M. M. (1985). Providing a more appropriate education for severely handicapped persons: Increasing and validating functional classroom tasks. *Journal of Applied Behavior Analysis, 18,* 289-301.

Reid, D. H., Schuh-Wear, C. L., & Brannon, M. E. (1978). Use of a group contingency to decrease staff absenteeism in a state institution. *Behavior Modification, 2,* 251-266.

Repp, A. C., & Deitz, D. E. D. (1979). Improving administrative-related staff behaviors at a state institution. *Mental Retardation, 17,* 185-192.

Shoemaker, J., & Reid, D. H. (1980). Decreasing chronic absenteeism among institutional staff: Effects of a low-cost attendance program. *Journal of Organizational Behavior Management, 2,* 317-328.

Shoemaker, J., & Reid, D. H. (1980). Increasing parental involvement with profoundly handicapped persons in an institutional setting. *Journal of Rehabilitation, 46,* 42-46.

Wilson, P. G., Reid, D. H., Phillips, J. F., & Burgio, L. D. (1984). Normalization of institutional mealtimes for profoundly retarded persons: Effects and noneffects of teaching family-style dining. *Journal of Applied Behavior Analysis, 17,* 189-201.

Chapter 3

INVOLVING HUMAN SERVICE STAFF IN APPLIED RESEARCH PROGRAMS

IN THE PRECEDING chapter it was stressed that in order to develop a successful research program in a human service agency, a senior researcher must work closely with other personnel indigenous to the agency. Otherwise, the senior researcher will most likely be unable to complete all the work that is required in a good research program. However, it was further noted that, typically, employees in human service agencies are not researchers based on their educational and training backgrounds, nor are they researchers based on their existing job classifications. Hence, successful involvement of agency personnel in research projects should not be taken for granted. Rather, their involvement should be specifically planned for and worked on as diligently as are any of the more traditional methodological aspects of conducting a research project. The purpose of this chapter is to discuss methods of successfully involving human service staff in research activities.

As also previously stressed, it is essential that any applied research undertaking within a human service agency be directed at fulfilling an existing agency responsibility — typically in terms of resolving a problem the agency is facing. This is particularly the case when planning how to involve agency staff in research programs. Staff already have a full-time job within the agency, and if their involvement in a research project requires a significant amount of time and effort beyond that required by their existing job responsibilities, their involvement in research activities is not likely to occur for very long. In addition, non-research staff are not as likely to be motivated initially to participate in research activities as the senior researcher due to not having had any previous (and enjoyable) experience in conducting research. Consequently, when attempting to involve human service agency staff in research activities, the first

35

step is to plan research projects that help staff fulfill their own existing responsibilities within the agency, albeit even if only on a somewhat indirect basis. Given the importance of tying research into agency service responsibilities of staff, exactly how agency personnel can become involved in applied research as part of their ongoing job is dependent in large part on the designated role that the senior researcher fulfills within the organizational structure of the agency.

Impact of the Organizational Role of the Senior Researcher on Methods of Involving Agency Staff in Research Projects

There are a variety of roles (i.e. job classifications and responsibilities) that senior researchers have in human service agencies, including administrative, supervisory and clinical. From the author's vantage point, the most useful role in terms of successfully involving other agency staff in research programs is a role that includes considerable supervisory and administrative authority. However, before discussing the merits of an authoritative-type role for an applied researcher relative to other agency roles, it should be noted that the specific job a senior researcher holds in a human service setting is not nearly as important as his/her willingness to put effort into research activity. As noted in Chapter 2, the best predictor of the success of a given research project, or a long-term program of research, is how hard the senior researcher is willing to work; the more work directed toward research, the more likely it is that the research will be successful. Hence, although the role a senior researcher fulfills within a human service agency can certainly facilitate or limit the amount of successful research conducted, research can be completed within essentially any role a senior researcher holds if he/she is willing to work diligently.

Senior Researcher in an Authoritative Role

An authoritative role in most human service agencies usually means that an individual is in an upper-level management position within the agency's organizational structure. Upper-level management roles typically involve supervisory responsibilities over one or more layers of staff positions. Authoritative-type jobs also entail related administrative authority that is necessary to fulfill the supervisory requirements (e.g. partial or full budgetary control, assignment of staff work schedules, hiring and firing of staff). To illustrate, a senior researcher may be employed as a school principal, a department head over a clinical unit in an institutional facility for the mentally retarded such as Director of Psychological Services or Director of Special Education, an assistant director for a community mental health agency with designated responsibility over several departmental units, an executive director over a private school, or a director of a preschool.

There are a number of advantages of a senior researcher's functioning in an authoritative role in a human service setting. First, these types of management positions usually are rather integral to a large portion of an agency's overall functioning. The ongoing job demands inherent in an authoritative position essentially ensure that the senior researcher is aware of key problems the agency is facing—problems whose resolution would make good applied research topics. By working on the day-to-day duties that the management and administrative role demands, the senior researcher should have no difficulty whatsoever generating a lengthy problem list (Chap. 2) from which to select relevant research questions. Relatedly, due to the job demands that the senior researcher/manager faces on a daily basis, it is unlikely that the senior researcher would bring on extra work for him/herself by attempting to focus on research programs that are unrelated to agency service obligations. In short, by being employed in an authoritative position, an applied researcher is more likely to select research topics that focus on relevant agency problems than if he/she is employed in other positions in the agency. Of course, it is essential that the senior researcher be able to competently fulfill the *service* function of the authoritative role independent of any research activity, albeit undoubtedly not perfectly. It is far beyond the scope of this text to describe what a professional in an authoritative position in a human service agency must do to proficiently fulfill respective agency responsibilities. Suffice it to say here that if a senior researcher does not fulfill an authoritative role with at least a reasonable degree of competence, then the individual essentially has no business engaging in research activity (and actually has no business being in an authoritative role regardless of any research involvement). The rationale for such an assertion goes back to one of the basic premises underlying this entire text: the first priority of all staff in human service agencies (including senior researchers) is fulfilling agency service obligations.

The second advantage of a senior researcher working in an authoritative position is due to the nature of the position: it carries authority. Hence, the senior researcher is in a situation to make important decisions that affect the involvement of other agency staff persons in research endeavors. Chapter 2, for example, described how a senior researcher can assist staff with their routine job responsibilities in order to facilitate their participation in applied research activities. Such assistance is facilitated considerably if the senior researcher has the authority to alter staff work assignments, although still ensuring that the routine service functions of staff are completed. If the senior researcher does not have authority over staff work responsibilites, he/she must negotiate at times with another supervisor or manager in order to involve agency staff in research—a process that, at best, is time consuming, and at worse, unsuccessful.

The authority aspect of the type of upper-level management position for a senior researcher that is emphasized here has a similar advantage to that just described that relates to the benefits of applied research. Specifically, relative to other types of positions in human service agencies, if an applied researcher is employed in an authoritative position, he/she is more likely to be able to ensure that whatever information is obtained from a given research project is actually used to enhance the agency's routine operation. In some situations, practitioners who conduct an applied research project face the same obstacles that researchers who are external to a respective agency encounter, in that the beneficial results of a project are not incorporated into the agency's functioning once the project has been terminated. For example, a research program might successfully demonstrate how to teach a novel leisure skill to institutionalized mentally retarded adults; yet, once the research project is over, the adult participants are never provided with the opportunity to actually use the newly acquired skill (e.g. necessary leisure materials are not made available, staff assistance that might be needed to help the clients initiate a prerequisite activity is not provided). Similarly, a more efficient means of teaching an arithmetic skill to elementary students relative to an existing teaching strategy may be developed in a research project, but certain teachers never adopt the new approach as part of their classroom instruction.

The reasons why potentially helpful information that results from an applied research project conducted by staff in a human service agency is never really utilized by the agency are varied. In some cases, other agency staff members are not convinced that the information obtained from the agency researchers' project is very useful. In other cases, the information from the research activity cannot be used during routine agency operations because the research methodology required extra resources (e.g. additional staff, specialized equipment) that are not available for day-to-day application within the agency. Additionally, the staff researchers may have made no attempt to routinely apply the results of their investigation once the formal study was completed. Each of these types of problematic situations, as well as most of the other factors that prohibit an agency from benefitting from a research endeavor, can be overcome by a senior researcher if he/she is employed in an authoritative position within the agency. The management authority inherent in such a role allows a researcher the control of agency staff assignments and resource allocation that is often needed to make necessary changes in order to incorporate useful research findings into agency operations on a routine basis.

A fourth advantage of a senior researcher being employed in an authoritative role within a human service agency pertains to a frequent problem that applied researchers need to avoid, or actually overcome, depending on the past experience of a given human service agency with researchers. Specifically, a researcher must avoid creating the impression on staff that he/she is only working in the agency to do research and is not to be bothered with the commonplace duties and problems of the agency. When staff view a researcher in this light, their general acceptance of the researcher and subsequent cooperation in research endeavors is likely to be considerably less than optimal. This type of problem is not likely to arise very often if a senior researcher is employed in an authoritative role in an agency and overtly deals with the agency's (and staff's) service demands on a day-to-day basis.

A related type of problem that occurs with researchers in applied settings that can be overcome through employment in an authoritative role is the impression formed among staff that the researcher is only concerned about improving his/her professional stature through research activity. Such an impression of researchers is frequently prevalent among all levels of staff in numerous applied settings, including clinicians, middle managers and executive directors. Unfortunately, in many cases, this rather negative opinion of researchers has been wellfounded based on past experiences human service agencies have had with researchers who have entered an agency with the sole purpose of conducting research — typically coming from a nearby college or university.

The negative impression that researchers sometimes have on an agency is not something that is necessarily discussed with the researcher or the researchers' operating base (e.g. the university) by representatives of a human service agency. Consequently, a researcher is often unaware of his/her reputation within a given human service agency. For example, agency directors frequently do not want to risk creating publicly viewed ill will with a local university with whom a researcher is affiliated by expressing displeasure about a professional researcher's activities. Nevertheless, the negative impression created by many university-based researchers typically has a strong within-agency focus; something that all levels of staff tend to group together and, at least implicitly, agree to complain about. An "us-versus-them" attitude then develops within the agency, with the "us" being the agency staff and the "them" being outside researchers. This type of situation can make it very difficult for a researcher to be successful in conducting applied research in human service settings because of resistive activities that staff will engage in as exemplified in Chapter 2. The negative reactions of staff also tend to leave an unfavorable impression on the university-based researcher and his/her university colleagues regarding the staff in a human service agency. That is, at times the "outside" researcher ends up devaluing the agency staff because they are uncooperative with the former's research efforts, giving the researcher the opinion that staff in non-academic human service settings are not progressively minded and not interested in advancing a professional field or the agency's own service provision via participation in research. Complaints about staff in applied settings being non-progressive or non-interested in research are relatively commonplace among many university faculty members. What the latter individuals fail to realize at times, however, is that it is their performance and attitude when interacting within human service agencies that frequently plays a large part in fostering some of the noted problems among agency staff.

If the senior researcher is in an authoritative position within the agency and his/her resulting work efforts at fulfilling agency service responsibilities are apparent to other agency staff persons, then the type of negative view of "outside" researchers as just noted is not likely to be a serious problem. Because of the senior researcher's continued day-to-day work performance, he/she is viewed more as a permanent part of the agency and not a temporary "white knight" who will vanish once a given research project is over. If the senior researcher performs his/her role competently (or at least diligently), because of the nature of most authoritative jobs in human service agencies, the effort that the senior researcher puts into agency services and his/her resulting contribution to the agency will generally be apparent, which, in turn, puts the researcher in a well-respected light among a number of staff. Being professionally respected among agency staff certainly facilitates research activity by the senior researcher relative to being viewed in a generally negative manner.

In considering the role of an applied researcher in an upper-level administrative or management position, a concern that often arises is whether the job demands of the position will allow the researcher sufficient time to conduct research. Because of the supervisory and/or administrative responsibility over a number of staff and clients inherent in authoritative positions, the amount and importance of the service demands of the job can often seem somewhat overwhelming to both the senior researcher and other staff—much less when research activities are added to the service responsibilities. Indeed, despite the advantages of a senior researcher being employed in an authoritative role as just discussed, this type of role for a researcher in an applied setting is somewhat controversial among researchers. The controversy is due to the effortful nature and stress-related responsibilities of this type of job, and many professionals believe that a researcher should avoid such a position because the service-demands disallow time and energy for research.

The concerns over the service-demands of an authoritative-type position are in large part well founded. Undoubtedly, if a senior researcher approaches the job sincerely, then the routine, day-to-day demands of an upper-level management position are usually quite heavy. A seemingly endless amount of unplanned demands also can arise on any given work day that make serious involvement in research seem impossible. Unplanned events that can unexpectedly take total control of a manager's workday or work-week and disallow time for research may include, for example, dealing with grievances from disgruntled employees, impromptu agency surveys by governmental regulatory bodies, lawsuits, and unexpected staff resignations, to name a few. Nevertheless, an authoritative position still seems most advantageous in terms of developing and maintaining a good research program. In this regard, it must be remembered that being an effective researcher in an applied setting is hard work. It is not an easy task, regardless of the service role the researcher fulfills in the agency. Also, despite the job demands of an authoritative position in an agency, the authority and resource control of such a position can actually *lessen* the senior researcher's efforts involved in developing a research program. The authoritative aspect of the position can facilitate the helpful involvement of other agency staff in research activities in order to share the research work load, because the senior researcher can control certain aspects of other staff persons' job responsibilities.

An additional concern of a senior researcher functioning within an authoritative role is that the researcher will lose his/her professional identity. Because the senior researcher will often spend the vast majority of work time on administrative and management issues, there will be little time for practicing the types of professional and/or clinical activities that the senior researcher was trained to do and what people in the senior researcher's profession typically do. Probably, the most common example of this situation is an individual who is trained to provide client therapy and conduct research as a Ph.D.-level psychologist and then assumes an authoritative job role in a human service agency. In the latter role, the psychologist really is not expected, nor paid, to provide client therapy or conduct research; he/she is paid to be an administrator and/or manager.

The potential loss of a senior researcher's professional identity because of employment in an authoritative position in a human service agency is, indeed, a serious consideration. Clearly, if a psychologist sincerely wants to spend the majority of work time providing, for example, client therapy, he/she should seek employment as a clinician and not as a manager or administrator. In many cases, though, an individual clinician can impact client clinical services more significantly if the clinician assumes an authoritative role and then has the necessary control to arrange for wide-scale improvements in client services by affecting how other clinicians perform their clinical duties. Also, being in an authoritative role does not necessarily require a loss of professional identity in terms of conducting research; as this text is attempting to demonstrate, authoritative positions can represent excellent opportunities for professionals to conduct research. Actually, conducting and disseminating research is one way of *maintaining and/or fostering* the professional identity of a professional who functions in an administrative or management role. Research activity, particularly in clinical areas, forces the senior researcher to maintain a current knowledge base of what is happening in a respective professional field and also sets the occasion for the senior researcher to interact with other professionals around the country who are leaders in the field. (See Chapter 7 for elaboration on how research can enhance professional interactions.)

Senior Researcher in a Designated Resource/Research Role

Although the authoritative-type role of a senior researcher as just discussed is, from the author's standpoint, the most advantageous role for developing and maintaining a research program in a human service setting, it is not the most common role for a researcher in an applied setting. Rather, the more usual role (at least within those human service settings that formally recognize research functions) is a designated resource/research role. In this type of position, a senior researcher is employed in a capacity within an agency that is specifically designated to conduct research. A resource/research position typically has no administrative, supervisory or clinical responsibilities other than research. The advantage, and rationale, of this type of agency role for a senior researcher is that the researcher is free from other job demands and can devote his/her entire time to research. In addition, it is generally expected that by being an agency-recognized research expert in a human service field, the senior researcher can function as a resource for other agency staff to assist them in conducting research if they are so interested.

Although the designated resource/research role for a senior researcher is a relatively popular model among professionals who want to establish a research program in a human service setting, in the long run it generally is not very effective. The disadvantages of this type of role in essence represent the converse of the advantages of the upper-level authoritative role of a senior researcher. To illustrate, by the nature of the resource model, the senior researcher is not in a position that is very integral to the day-to-day functioning and problems of a human service agency. A senior researcher in a resource role is usually not consulted, much less intimately involved, in efforts to resolve major problems that the agency is facing. Consequently, the familiarity of the senior researcher with the routine problems of the agency is typically not very astute and/or relevant, and the ability of the researcher to design applied research programs that effectively resolve agency problems is seriously hampered. Relatedly, the "us-versus-them" attitude noted earlier that often develops between a university-based researcher and an agency's staff frequently develops between a senior researcher in a resource role and the rest of the staff in the human service agency. This type of attitude among staff is usually initiated because, when the senior researcher attempts to work with staff, the topic of the intended research is selected by the researcher without any serious involvement of the staff. As a result, the intended research represents primarily or exclusively a concern of the applied researcher and not of the staff, and the research work is viewed by staff as being somewhat unimportant or irrelevant for their jobs as well as representing undesired extra work for the staff who are expected to be involved in the research project.

Despite the typical problems of the designated resource/research role, the idea of having a significant amount of time specifically designated to conduct applied research is quite appealing. One method of compromising between the advantages and disadvantages of the resource/research role is to designate a major part of an agency staff position as a resource/research function and define the remainder of the role in an agency service capacity (e.g. an authoritative or clinical position). In the latter situation, expectations and time designation for doing research remain (although on a reduced level) and some of the problems of not being integrally involved in the agency's routine service provision and of being viewed as an "outsider" by staff are diminished. This type of split role is exemplified by the position held by Jim Favell at Western Carolina Center. Jim is the Center's Director of Research and functions in a designated research/resource role. However, Jim also oversees, through an organizational chain of comand, the operation of a residential living unit for non-ambulatory, profoundly handicapped clients (cf. Risley & Favell, 1979).

Other Agency Roles for Applied Researchers

The two models just discussed in terms of agency roles for senior researchers represent either the most effective role or the most popular role. There are also two other common roles that researchers can fulfill in the organizational structure of an agency: clinical and middle management roles.

Researcher in a Clinical Role. Much has been discussed about the dual role of a professional as a clinician and an applied researcher. Although a number of benefits of this type of role have been proposed, it generally does not seem to work very well over the long run for several reasons. First and foremost, clinical positions such as a psychologist, teacher, speech pathologist, physical therapist, etc., typically do not have significant supervisory and/or administrative authority over any staff positions or agency resources. Hence, obtaining necessary assistance for conducting a successful research program can be quite difficult. Often, what happens when a clinician is serious about wanting to conduct research is that the clinician tries to conduct every aspect of a given research project by him/herself because it is difficult to obtain consistent staff assistance on a research endeavor, with the result that the clinician has a very effortful undertaking. Considerable effort and diligence is, of course, necessary to conduct any good research project in applied settings. However, in the situation described here, the work load easily becomes too excessive and the clinician/researcher cannot maintain the efforts for long periods of time. Hence, the research involvement is usually rather short-lived. The problematic situation also can (inadvertently) arise in which the clinician neglects his/her clinical responsibilities in order to conduct research. In the latter situation, not only are clients deprived of services, but staff become displeased and disrespectful of the clinician, which in turn creates an unpleasant and, eventually, unproductive work environment for the clinician/researcher. This type of situation is unfortunately relatively common in applied settings in which a clinician is attempting to conduct a serious research program.

Researcher in a Middle-Management Role. A middle-management role for a researcher refers to a position in a human service agency that has the same types of responsibilities and authority as the upper-management authoritative-type role described earlier but on a smaller scale. To illustrate, in a residential facility a middle-management position might be the supervisor of a residential building in which a given number of clients reside and receive services, whereas an upper-management position may be the director over all residential units (and supervisors). The advantages of a senior researcher functioning in a middle-management role are basically the same as those associated with an upper-level authoritative position but, again, of a reduced scale. A middle manager, for example, has supervisory control over agency staff and resources as does an upper-level manager, but the former has control over a smaller number of staff and resources than the latter.

In contrast to a senior-level management position, the disadvantages of a senior researcher functioning in a middle-management role are rather numerous. First, due to the smaller span of responsibility and potential control of a middle manager relative to a senior manager, the types of agency problems that the middle manager faces that could represent topics for applied research are more limited (although in many agencies, middle managers face enough serious problems to keep an applied researcher busy for an extended period of time). Second (and this problem is shared with upper-level management roles), middle managers are often in a demanding job situation that can render time and effort directed at research difficult (but not impossible). Relatedly, the middle manager often has less control over his/her job responsibilities than a senior manager, because the former has more superiors who provide directions as to what the middle manager must do. Whereas an upper-level manager receives directions usually from only one superior, a middle-level manager receives directions from several superiors through the organizational chain of command. A final disadvantage of a middle-management role is that in many cases, human service agencies simply do not provide a high enough salary for middle-management positions to be competitive for a senior researcher type person. For example, often Ph.D. psychologists can make considerably more money when employed by a human service agency as a professional clinician in contrast to a middle manager, even though the latter position is better suited for conducting an applied research program.

Impact of the Organizational Role of Agency Staff Members on Methods of Involving Staff in Research Programs

In addition to the impact of the role that a senior researcher holds within a human service agency on the involvement of agency staff in research, the roles that staff fulfill can also have an important impact. For example, although a middle-management role is not particularly advantageous for a senior researcher as just described, this type of role can be quite desirable for a *research colleague* for a senior researcher. Because staff in middle-management positions have designated authority over some staff and resources, that authority can place those individuals in strategic situations to bring about significant resolutions to certain agency problems through applied investigations under the research direction of the senior researcher. A good example of how a middle manager can be a successful research colleague is represented by the research conducted by Maureen Schepis. As a supervisor over a small living unit for institutionalized developmentally disabled children and adolescents, Maureen was instrumental in the success of applied research investigations directed at demonstrating methods of conducting non-vocal communication training with severely and profoundly mentally retarded persons (Faw et al., 1981) and at improving staff training and management procedures (Schepis et al., 1982). Similarly, in another middle-management job as director of an educational program within an institutional setting, Maureen played a key role in a research project directed at improving the efficiency of teaching procedures with severely handicapped persons (Schepis, Reid, & Fitzgerald, 1987).

Another agency role that can be advantageous for potential research colleagues of a senior researcher is somewhat analogous to the designated research/resource role noted previously. In essence, this type of role can function as an applied research assistant for the senior researcher. Research assistant positions are very uncommon in typical human service settings as are all research-related positions in those settings. However, research assistant type positions can be arranged in human service agencies without too much difficulty if several guidelines are followed. First, it is almost imperative that a senior researcher be in an upper-level authoritative position in order to have the authority to take the necessary administrative and personnel actions to create a research assistant type position. Second, because staff resources are somewhat limited in a number of human service agencies, in many cases it is easier to arrange for a research assistant position (and to justify its existence) on a part-time basis in contrast to full-time. Similarly, it is essential that the research assistant position, once established, be assigned to only those projects that *clearly and visibly* assist an agency's service provision in order to help justify the position relative to using the position in a more direct service-related role within the agency. By focusing a research assistant's efforts overtly on important agency problems, other staff within the agency are more likely to be responsive to the person in that position than if efforts are directed to research topics that do not clearly address an agency problem.

Employing the guidelines just noted, a part-time research position can be particularly valuable in helping a senior researcher focus on *large-scale, long-term* research programs. Comprehensive research undertakings that persist for several years can greatly improve an agency's operation. Frequently, a senior researcher would really not have the time to attend to this type of research undertaking on a consistent basis without the help of an assistant because of the time required of the senior researcher to solve the more routine day-to-day agency problems. (See Chapter 6 for a discussion of ways of developing a long-term program of research in addition to the use of research assistants.)

Although the designated resource/research role for a senior researcher has a lot of disadvantages as described earlier, such disadvantages do not exist with a research assistant position even though the positions appear to operate similarly. The reason that the same disadvantages do not exist with the latter type of position is that if the senior researcher competently fulfills his/her authoritative role within a human service agency, then the research assistant position is generally viewed as an extension of the senior researcher's authoritative role, with the accompanying desirable characteristics of that role. Actually, a "research assistant" title is somewhat misleading in this regard because of the non-applied, more traditional experimental responsibilities that such a title usually is assumed to imply. More appropriate titles (and ones that usually are better received among agency staff) would be along the lines of a Program Evaluator or Program Development Specialist. The latter titles better describe what the role is expected to do in terms of helping to improve a (program) component of a human service agency's functioning (through applied research with the guidance of the senior researcher).

In many ways, the most readily available role for potential research colleagues for a senior researcher is a clinical role. Essentially, all human service agencies employ clinicians, be they psychologists, speech pathologists, recreators, teachers or occupational therapists. As discussed in Chapter 2, there is an endless array of important clinical problems that could be addressed through applied research. Although clinicians usually cannot function as a *senior researcher* in a research program as noted earlier, a clinician can often function as a *co-experimenter* with a senior researcher. In particular, a clinician is in a very advantageous position to function as a treatment intervener (i.e. the person who conducts the problem-solving intervention part of a research project) in clinically oriented research projects while simultaneously conducting normal clinical duties with an agency's clients.

In essence, many existing roles in human service settings are advantageous for research colleagues to fulfill. All things considered, probably the most important ingredient in successfully involving agency staff members in applied research endeavors with a senior researcher in regard to the agency role that a staff person fulfills is selecting a research topic that allows a staff member to function within his/her routine job capacity while simultaneosly working on a research activity (Chap. 2). Relatedly, there are *specific types* of research undertakings for research colleagues that are especially amenable to different types of staff roles. Selecting and/or designing research projects that are differentially advantageous according to the particular role that a staff person fulfills are discussed in greater detail in Chapter 5. However, as discussed in the next section, there are also some personal characteristics of staff members within human service agencies that are important in selecting productive research colleagues.

Selecting Research Colleagues Within an Agency: Advantageous Individual Characteristics

In determining whom a senior researcher should involve in the integral parts of an applied research project, an analogy from the athletic world can be helpful. A traditional adage in football is that when a coach must decide what offensive play to call in light of a game-deciding situation, the approach with the most consistent probability of success is to give the football to the best running back on the team and have him run behind the best blocker on the team. In short, when good results are crucial, a coach should rely on his/her best personnel. The same situation exists when determining whom to involve in a research project in a human service agency: *for best research results, a senior researcher should work with the most proficient staff in the agency on a collaborative basis.*

The rationale for selecting the most competent staff as research colleagues for the senior researcher is basically straightforward. Essentially, the same skill and diligence that cause certain staff members to stand out within an agency on a day-to-day basis as being particularly competent will carry over to their involvement in research activities. Of course, attempting to work with representatives from an agency's most proficient core of staff requires that an applied researcher be able to determine *who* the most proficient staff persons are among the agency's staff population. Such a determination is usually quite simple if the senior researcher is functioning in an integral position within the agency's work force, such as in an upper-level management position. It is usually very apparent to senior managers which of their staff are functioning most competently. In contrast, if an applied researcher is employed in a resource type of position, he/she does not always have firsthand knowledge regarding which staff members perform their roles most proficiently. In the latter type of position, a researcher must rely on only indirect impressions about staff competence such as what people say about a given staff member or how a staff member responds in an interview—indices of performance that often are not very reliable.

In selecting skilled staff persons to collaborate with on a research program, a mistake that is often made by applied researchers is to overemphasize the importance of behavior-modification skills among staff. Because the senior researcher is behaviorally oriented (at least as far as the focus of this text), the tendency is to gravitate toward other persons in the agency who are relatively skilled behavior modifiers. Skills in behavior modification clearly are an asset for applied research colleagues. However, skills in behavior modification represent only one subset of all the skills necessary for a staff person to function effectively as a research colleague. Actually, skills in behavior modification should be placed relatively low on the continuum of important skills among people who are potential research partners. Table 1 lists the priority characteristics of agency staff persons who are most likely to successfully function as research colleagues for a senior researcher.

Table 1

Prioritized Characteristics of Personnel Likely to be Good Research Collaborators

Priority	Characteristic
1st	Sincere concern about client welfare
2nd	Diligent in performing existing job
3rd	Interpersonally pleasant
4th	Skilled in behavior modification
5th	Experienced in applied research

The first priority in selecting a staff member to be a collaborator on an applied research project is that the individual should be sincerely concerned about client welfare. The point here is that the senior researcher must never lose sight of his/her first priority: the agency's service provision to its clients. By selecting research partners who are sincerely interested in client welfare, the probability that the concern for clients will remain a top priority throughout all aspects of the research undertaking is enhanced tremendously. Unfortunately, objectively determining who is truly concerned about client welfare (as well as determining who meets several of the other criteria for staff research collaborators to be discussed) is not always straightforward. It is beyond the scope of this text to describe how to make such determinations; at this point it must be left to the individual judgment of the senior researcher.

The second most important characteristic of a good research colleague is diligence. As stated repeatedly, good applied research in human service settings requires a very considerable amount of hard work. Agency staff members who consistently demonstrate diligence in performing their routine job duties are much more likely to be diligent research colleagues than are staff members who perform in a less effortful manner. Diligent staff members also are usually well respected among an agency's general staff population. Consequently, the involvement of hard-working staff in applied research programs can facilitate a favorable impression among other staff regarding the research activities that the former are involved in relative to the involvement of agency staff who are less respected because of a commonly viewed lack of work effort.

The third priority skill for an agency research colleague is interpersonal effectiveness — the ability to get along with people. The focus on selecting research co-workers who consistently interact with other people in a pleasant manner is due to two primary reasons. First, usually staff members whom other people in an agency generally like to be around, because they are, in essence, friendly, are more likely to accomplish the goals of the research project when such goals involve being able to work with other agency staff. Second, working with people who are pleasant to be around makes the research work inherently more *fun* for the senior researcher, as well as for his/her other research colleagues. Because research does require hard and patient work, the more that can be done to make the work enjoyable, then the more likely it is that staff and the senior researcher will continue to perform the required work; one of the easiest ways to make research tasks enjoyable is to work with pleasant and friendly colleagues.

The fourth priority skill for a good research colleague is competence in behavior modification. Because applied research as discussed here has a behavioral orientation, the more behavioral skills the research colleagues have, then the less the senior researcher has to do him/herself and the less the senior researcher has to teach to other staff persons. The reason, however, that behavioral skills are not given a higher priority (a mistake noted earlier that is often made) is that such skills are considerably easier to teach to staff than are the higher priority skills just noted. Hence, a senior researcher should first seek to find a research partner who is sincerely concerned about client welfare, a diligent worker, and basically a pleasant person. These are attributes that usually are very difficult to teach to people. If a senior researcher works with staff members who display these characteristics *and* are skilled behavior modifiers, then the senior researcher is likely to have some outstanding colleagues; if such is not the case, then the senior researcher should strive to find people who have the first three attributes and then teach those persons the necessary behavior-modification skills.

The fifth important characteristic for research colleagues is experience in applied behavior analysis research. The value of research experience for a research colleague is essentially the same as the value of behavior-modification skills. Unfortunately, it is typically quite rare that a senior researcher will find a co-worker in a human service setting who has good skills in behavior analysis research, unless the senior researcher has previously collaborated with given staff members on several research projects. However, the skills necessary for co-workers to be able to conduct certain components of a research project that would be obtained through past experience in behavior analysis research can usually be taught by the senior researcher considerably easier than the first four types of priority skills just noted.

A final valuable characteristic of a good staff research collaborator that is not listed in Table 1 is *interest in research*. It is unlikely that any agency staff member will be a very productive research colleague for a senior researcher if the former is not interested in research. The reason, though, that interest in research is not listed as a priority characteristic in Table 1 is that it is not really expected that a senior researcher will find agency staff members who have such an interest. In most cases, staff in typical human service agencies have had no exposure to the type of applied, problem-solving research in which the senior researcher would like to involve the staff. Without any real knowledge about this type of research, agency staff cannot be realistically expected to have an interest in being involved in research activities. Consequently, the senior researcher should assume that he/she will need to *develop* an interest in research among staff members who are potential research collaborators.

Precisely describing how a senior researcher can develop interest in applied research among potential staff research colleagues is difficult. The difficulty is due to the *multi*-component process that is usually involved. In essence, many of the suggested operational strategies for conducting research discussed throughout this entire text pertain at least in part to developing a serious interest in research among agency staff. Involving staff in the selection of a research topic, for example, as well as ensuring that the research topic is directed at resolving an important problem facing a human service agency (and the staff), are important steps in this regard. Making research activities as enjoyable as possible (Chap. 6) and ensuring that staff receive the appropriate professional credit and rewards for their research involvement (Chap. 7) are also important components.

In addition to the different strategies discussed throughout this text as just exemplified, an important step (and usually the first step) in developing research interest among agency staff is to explain to staff what an applied, problem-solving research project entails. The goal in explaining the focus and method of problem-solving research is not to immediately evoke serious interest among staff members in terms of working on a research project with the senior researcher (although that would be a nice outcome). Rather, the goal is simply to convince the staff to be willing to give the research involvement a try. If the guidelines for conducting *successful* applied research that this text discusses are followed, then a more serious interest in research activities and eventually perhaps even a degree of excited interest is likely to develop among staff research collaborators over time.

Relevance of Job Classification to Staff Participation in Research

An issue that periodically arises when deciding which staff would be effective research collaborators for a senior researcher is the job classification of respective staff members. Typically, staff in human service agencies (particularly in state-operated agencies) are employed in positions that have a personnel classification scheme with an accompanying job description. Concern is generated when considering whether a given staff person's job description will allow for participation in applied research activities. The concern is based on the assumption (or written directive) that staff members must perform only those duties that are specified in the job description. Consequently, a senior researcher may decide not to approach certain staff members about collaborating on research, because the researcher knows that the staff person's job description does not include participation in research activities.

A certain degree of concern is indeed warranted over the job classification of agency staff members in regard to their involvement in research programs. However, often such concern is needlessly overexaggerated; senior researchers and other individuals attach too much importance to the role of the job description. In particular, if an agency staff person is involved in an applied research project that is aimed at resolving an important problem within the agency that a staff member is involved with (which is the type of problem-solving research that should be directed by the senior researcher), then the research participation of the staff person really is not very different than his/her involvement in performing routine job duties. Furthermore, if job descriptions were interpreted very precisely, much of what a typical staff member does on a day-to-day basis as part of the normal job routine would probably be disallowed, anyway. Nevertheless, in those cases where job descriptions do have a significant degree of control over what a staff person does on a day-to-day basis, then some specific action may be required by the senior researcher, because rarely do job descriptions in human service systems specify involvement in research activities. Probably, the easiest way to resolve the problem of a job description (potentially) disallowing a staff member's participation in applied research is to *change the job description*. If a senior researcher is employed in an authoritative position in a human service agency, he/she can probably change staff job descriptions with little difficulty, except for having to work through a paper-ladened bureaucratic process with the agency personnel office.

In essence, in most cases the job classification of prospective research co-workers should be considerably less of a concern than the priority characteristics of good research collaborators as presented in Table 1. Also, as noted earlier, if the guidelines for selecting a relevant research topic are followed as presented in Chapter 2, the involvement of human service staff in research projects will not really take the staff away from their existing job responsibilities. However, there are a few occasions when certain staff members might be asked to do some things as part of a research project that are indeed quite different from their usual duties. For example, to help determine how to teach appropriate dress styles to profoundly mentally retarded women as part of an applied research program, Hilda Gault in her role as a secretary was asked to help measure how well certain clothing selections chosen by the women were color-coordinated (Nutter & Reid, 1978). Similarly, Carole McNew in her secretarial role was asked to assist in determining the legibility of return-address stamps placed on envelopes by profoundly mentally retarded women as part of a research project aimed at determining an efficient means of teaching a remunerative work skill to the handicapped clients (Schepis et al., 1987). In these two examples, the secretaries were asked to provide assistance in a research project that involved activities that were certainly not specified in their job descriptions. A senior researcher can usually obtain this type of staff assistance on research projects if several guidelines are followed. First, the requested activities must be related to helping fulfill obvious service needs of the agency, even if the specific activities are not identified in a given job description; otherwise there is really no justification for the request for assistance. Second, the assistance should be provided on a volunteer basis; if a respective staff member is not interested in working on (research) activities that are not a clear part of his/her job description, it would be ill advised to mandate such assistance. Frequently, though, if the requested assistance is of a temporary nature and represents a somewhat novel break in the staff member's job routine, volunteer help is easy to obtain.

Employing and Supervising a Senior Researcher

The procedures that have been discussed throughout this chapter should be helpful to senior researchers in involving staff who are indigenous to a human service agency in applied research activities. Of course, for the recommended strategies to be helpful, there must be a *senior researcher type* person (Chap. 1) employed in the agency to direct the agency's research efforts. In cases where a human service agency does not have a person with the necessary applied research know-how to function as a senior researcher, then some additional steps are necessary if the agency's management desires to have applied research conducted within the agency.

If the executive or senior management body or some component thereof (e.g. one particular senior manager), of a human service agency intends to have an applied research program and there is no individual who has sufficient training and experience in research technology to function as a senior researcher, then there are essentially two strategies that can be used to develop a research program. One strategy is for an individual (e.g. the senior manager who is interested in applied research) to actively assume the responsibility of acquiring the skills necessary to function as a senior researcher. The second strategy is to recruit and employ a senior researcher type person within the human service agency and then oversee, and work with, that individual on applied research endeavors. The latter strategy is usually the more productive and, hence, will be focused on here. However, for various reasons—particularly, insufficient funding at times—it is not always possible for an agency to hire a senior researcher type professional. Because there is no alternative in such situations except to use the former approach if an applied research program is desired, a few comments will be provided regarding how a given agency staff member might go about acquiring technical research skills.

Self-Development of Applied Research Skills

Developing skills in applied research technology while working within a human service setting without having had any graduate-level training in research methodology is a difficult task. A major part of the difficulty is that the process is quite time consuming, especially when considering that a practitioner already has a full-time job within the agency. Furthermore, the individual must initiate and locate means of acquiring relevant information without any readily available, pre-specified course of action in this type of undertaking. Nevertheless, some professionals have indeed developed the necessary skills to conduct applied research as a senior researcher in a human service agency using their own self-initiative. This section describes some steps that a practitioner might take if he/she is seriously interested in developing applied research skills.

Similar to a basic ingredient in actually *conducting* an applied research program in a human service setting, probably the most important prerequisite for a practitioner to self-develop technical research skills is the willingness to put forth consistent effort. A considerable amount of diligence and perseverance is required for a practitioner to teach him/herself how to conduct sound applied behavioral research. In addition, a practitioner generally must be willing to work on acquiring technical research knowledge in large part on his/her own time (i.e., separate from the regularly scheduled work time within the agency) and at his/her own expense.

If a practitioner is sincere in being willing to put forth the effort to learn research skills, then the most advantageous process is to enroll in university or college classes that teach applied behavior analysis. Further, if a supervised practicum could be arranged as part of a class, then the practitioner is likely to have the opportunity to acquire a good knowledge base in applied research skills. Of course, to take advantage of this process, a univesity or college must be relatively close to a practitioner's human service agency and offer courses in applied behavior analysis by a competent behavior analyst. For practitioners who already have doctoral-level training in a human service field but lack training in applied behavior analysis per se, a related possibility for acquiring technical research skills in applied behavioral research is to seek a postdoctoral internship at a behaviorally oriented human service agency which is affiliated with a university program. In the latter case, the practitioner usually must be willing to relocate for six months to a year, as well as accept a significant reduction in income during the postdoctorate appointment.

If enrolling in formal classes or training programs in behavior analysis is not a feasible option for a practitioner, then he/she must assume total responsibility for acquiring the necessary knowledge without the benefit of a designated teacher or mentor. Probably, the best place to start with such a process is to read several textbooks on applied behavior analysis. A number of texts exist from which to choose, with perhaps the most useful ones (from the viewpoint of the author of this text) being

Bailey and Bostow's (1979) *Research Methods In Applied Behavior Analysis* and Alberto and Troutman's (1982) *Applied Behavior Analysis for Teachers: Influencing Student Performance.* Other texts that would be helpful, although somewhat more difficult to comprehend, include Kazdin's (1982) *Single-Case Research Designs: Methods for Clinical and Applied Settings* and Barlow and Hersen's (1984) *Single Case Experimental Designs: Strategies for Studying Behavior Change (2nd ed.).*

Concurrently with studying textbooks, a practitioner should regularly study journal articles in applied behavior analysis that relate to his/her particular area of responsibility and interest in the human services. The *Journal of Applied Behavior Analysis* generally is the most helpful in regard to behavior analysis research methodology, although there are a number of other journals that also publish good applied behavioral research that are useful (see Table 2 in Chapter 7 and Appendix B for sample journals). Attending relevant professional conferences can also be beneficial. (See Chapters 6 and 7 regarding methods of selecting and utilizing conferences and conventions for professional development.)

If a practitioner can obtain an initial knowledge base about applied behavioral research through the rather academic types of activities just noted, then the individual should attempt some small-scale applied behavior-analysis projects within his/her human service agency. Preferably, the projects should be undertaken in collaboration with someone else who has at least some initial knowledge about applied behavior analysis, be it an agency colleague, a university faculty member or a graduate student. By working with another research-interested person, the practitioner will have more of an opportunity to acquire new information as well as receive constructive feedback as various projects are developed and implemented. Once a practitioner proceeds to the point of actually conducting applied behavior analysis activities (albeit initially on a simple and small-scale basis), then the practitioner is really well on his/her way to acquiring the necessary skills to eventually function as a senior researcher in a human service agency. At that point (assuming that the types of academically related self-teaching practices noted earlier continue), the procedures discussed throughout this text for conducting applied research in human service agencies should become relevant for the practitioner.

Selecting and Supervising a Senior Researcher

Because primarily of the very significant amount of effort and time involved in the process of self-developing skills in applied behavioral research as just summarized, it is usually more effective (or at least more efficient) for an agency's management to recruit and employ a senior researcher if an applied research program is desired within a human service agency. Fortunately, in this regard, as noted earlier in Chapter 1, there is currently a relatively large number of professionals who have been trained in applied behavior analysis and, subsequently, could be employed in a respective agency as a senior researcher. Given the large pool of potential senior researchers, the issue facing the management component of a human service agency is, in essence, how to select a senior researcher who will work well with the staff and clients of a particular agency.

Determining how to select a professional employee from an applicant pool who will perform proficiently in a given job role has been the subject of numerous discussions and research over the years. All things considered though, despite the attention given to this issue historically, there is really no way to predict for sure which applicant will turn out to be a competent employee. However, using a few basic guidelines, managerial or supervisory personnel within a human service agency can at least increase the probability of selecting an individual who will eventually succeed in the role of a senior researcher.

As with selecting an employee for essentially any type of job capacity, the best indicator of whether or not a given applicant will succeed as a senior researcher is the applicant's past performance: the better the individual's performance has been in fulfilling the specific types of responsibilities that will be expected of a senior researcher in a human service agency, the more likely it is that the individual will perform satisfactorily in the latter position. Hence, an agency supervisor should seek to employ a practitioner who has successfully functioned as a senior researcher in a similar type of human service setting as the supervisor's agency. To achieve such a goal generally means that the supervisor must have a job situation that will attract an experienced researcher/practitioner from another human service agency. Consequently, employing this type of person as a senior researcher will probably be somewhat costly for an agency, in that the agency will most likely have to offer a more lucrative salary than what the experienced senior researcher is currently receiving, or a more productive and/or pleasant working environment, or a more desirable geographic living arrangement, etc.

If an agency's management is unable or unwilling to recruit and employ an experienced and successful senior researcher from another human service agency, then the agency should seek to obtain a person who comes as close as possible to having had some type of experience in successfully performing the types of duties that will be expected. In particular, because it is essential that at least one practitioner in a human service agency be skilled in the technical aspects of applied research if the agency is to successfully involve its staff in a research program, it is crucial that the prospective senior researcher be experienced in successfully completing research activities (i.e. be a published author of an applied research article). In short, to really be a strong applicant for a senior researcher role, an individual must have successfully completed the entire multi-step process of designing, implementing ad writing up an applied research project. Otherwise, there is no way to be sure that the applicant has the necessary skills to be a senior researcher. It is also most advantageous that the applicant have some experience in successfully completing a research project *independently,* or at least with only minimal guidance from a more experienced applied researcher.

In addition to having experience in publishing research, a good applicant for a senior researcher position should have experience in the *right kind* of research: applied behavior analysis. Because of the disadvantageous role of basic experimentation in human service settings as described in Chapter 1, experience in conducting non-applied research is not really an asset for a prospective senior researcher. A number of human service executives have made the mistake, at least in terms of developing a strong applied research program in a human service setting, of employing an individual who is trained in (only) basic research methodology. Quite frequently, individuals trained in basic experimentation do not have the appropriate skills (and perhaps more importantly not the appropriate interest) to conduct applied, problem-solving research within the typical environment of a human service agency. Actually, in a number of cases, doctoral-level professionals with a basic research background (and no real applied experience) have become employed in human service settings, not because they desired that type of position, but, rather, due to relative necessity, because comparably paid positions for basic researchers have become relatively rare. The result of such a process generally has not been very beneficial for the agency or the basic researcher in the long run. In short, if the only applicants for a senior researcher position are individuals versed in basic research skills, then overall it would be wiser for an agency's management to seek to develop an applied research program by using the approach summarized in the preceding section of encouraging a current agency practitioner to self-develop the necessary research expertise.

It is usually relatively easy for a supervisor to determine if a prospective senior researcher's skills (and interest) are in basic versus applied research. Most relevant in this regard would be the research article(s) previously published by the applicant. A quick review of the published paper(s) will indicate whether or not the individual's approach to research involves resolving a problem of immediate social relevance in the human service profession. In addition, denoting an applicant's research interests through an interview process can be informative in terms of soliciting ideas on the *types* of research projects (i.e. basic versus applied) the individual would like to conduct if he/she was employed in a given human service agency. If an applicant indicates an interest in problem-solving research, it can also be useful to solicit ideas on how he/she might go about addressing a specific problem that exists in the agency from an applied research perspective. The most important information to obtain in the latter situation is whether or not the applicant seems to know how to design a research project such that it could be feasibly conducted within the normal operating practices of the human service agency (for example, through the use of certain methodological features that are amenable to applied settings as discussed in Chapter 5).

Once a prospective senior researcher is identified who has appropriate credentials in applied behavioral research, then other characteristics of the applicant must be reviewed. In particular, the priority characteristics described earlier (Table 1) for staff research collaborators in a human service agency should be considered. If an applicant appears to fulfill the criteria of having a sincere interest in client welfare, performing job duties in a diligent manner (which usually can be ascertained by talking to the applicant's previous supervisors or mentors) and interacting well with peers and colleagues, then the applicant stands a very good chance of being a successful senior researcher for the human service agency. However, because of the different roles of a senior researcher versus agency staff research collaborators, in that the former must be considerably more skilled in applied research technology, the relative importance of the priority characteristics are different for a senior researcher. Specifically, skills in applied behavior analysis research and behavior modification should be the top-priority skills for a senior researcher; the other characteristic skills should come after research and behavior modification in priority.

After an applicant is selected to fill a senior researcher role, the management of a human service agency must determine how to specifically utilize the individual within the agency's service operation. Such a decision should, of course, be based on what the existing needs of the agency are as well as what the specific human service specialty of the senior researcher is (e.g. psychology, special education, administration/management). If the basic premise of this chapter is followed, the agency would seek to employ the senior researcher in a relevant upper-level authoritative role. If an authoritative position is not currently possible, then management should seek to employ the senior researcher in a middle-management position or a research/resource role within the agency. Once the senior researcher assumes one of these types of positions, then the other approaches discussed in this chapter as well as in the rest of this text become relevant for assisting the senior researcher (and his/her supervisor) in successfully developing a program of applied research within the agency.

REFERENCES

Alberto, P. A., & Troutman, A. C. (1982). *Applied behavior analysis for teachers: Influencing student performance.* Columbus, OH: Charles E. Merrill.

Bailey, J. S., & Bostow, D. E. (1979). *Research methods in applied behavior analysis.* Tallahassee, FL: Copy Grafix.

Barlow, D. H., & Hersen, M. (1984). *Single case experimental designs: Strategies for studying behavior change.* New York: Pergamom Press.

Faw, G. D., Reid, D. H., Schepis, M. M., Fitzgerald, J. R., & Welty, P. A. (1981). Involving institutional staff in the development and maintenance of sign language skills with profoundly retarded persons. *Journal of Applied Behavior Analysis, 14,* 411-423.

Kazdin, A. E. (1982). *Single case research designs: Methods for clinical and applied settings.* New York: Oxford University Press.

Nutter, D., & Reid, D. H. (1978). Teaching retarded women a clothing selection skill using community norms. *Journal of Applied Behavior Analysis, 11,* 475-487.

Risley, T. R., & Favell, J. (1979). Constructing a living environment in an institution. In L. A. Hamerlynk (Ed.): *Behavioral systems for the developmentally disabled: II. Institutional, clinic, and community environments.* New York: Brunner/Mazel.

Schepis, M. M., Reid, D. H., & Fitzgerald, J. R. (1987). A group instruction program for teaching a remunerative work skill to profoundly retarded persons: Acquisition, generalization and maintenance. *Journal of Applied Behavior Analysis,* in press.

Schepis, M. M., Reid, D. H., Fitzgerald, J. R., Faw, G. D., van den Pol, R. A., & Welty, P. A. (1982). A program for increasing manual signing by autistic and profoundly retarded youth within the daily environment. *Journal of Applied Behavior Analysis, 15,* 363-379.

Chapter 4

OBTAINING SUPERVISORY AND EXTERNAL AGENCY SUPPORT FOR RESEARCH

IN THE PRECEDING chapters the importance of an applied researcher working closely with his/her staff was stressed. Effective staff involvement in research activity is a critical, if not essential, element in the development of a successful applied research program by a senior researcher. However, there is another contingent within typical human service agencies with whom a senior researcher should strive to establish an effective working relationship if he/she is going to be very successful at conducting applied research: supervisory personnel. In addition, knowing how to use financial and/or personnel support from sources external to a senior researcher's human service agency can be very beneficial. This chapter discusses methods of obtaining effective supervisory and external agency support for applied research, as well as some common pitfalls to avoid in the process.

Obtaining Supervisory Support

Depending on the orientation of the top-level executive(s) in a human service agency, obtaining supervisory support for an applied researcher's investigative endeavors can have different meanings. Because a supervisor's views on research can affect how a senior researcher should go about conducting investigations, several typical supervisory orientations will be briefly reviewed here. Probably, the ideal situation in this regard is for an applied researcher to work in a human service setting under a director who actively encourages and/or directs his/her agency staff to conduct research. Iverson Riddle has taken such an approach as Director of Western Carolina Center and, consequently, it is not surprising that his residential center for developmentally disabled persons has consistently conducted successful research in a variety of service-related areas, including, for example, early intervention (Dunst, 1985), reduction of behavior disorders (Favell, McGimsey, & Schell, 1982), and improvement of educational and training technologies (Green, et al., 1986, Realon, et al., 1986; Schepis, Reid & Fitzgerald, 1987). Unfortunately, however (at least in regard to the task of an applied researcher), human service agencies are rarely directed by individuals who actively promote research.

If an agency director does not actively encourage research activity, then the next most desirable situation in terms of supervisory support for a senior researcher is a director who has at least some appreciation for the value of research. That is, a supervisor may not really do anything to encourage research, but he/she respects the efforts of others who do engage in research activity. This type of supervisory orientation toward research is probably the most common among human service agency executives. Finally, a less common but nevertheless relatively pervasive supervisory orientation toward research is an approach that involves overtly *denouncing* the role of research in human service settings and prohibiting or discouraging agency staff from participating in research.

If a senior researcher works within an agency with a supervisor or director who has the first orientation toward research just described (that of actively promoting research), then no explicit steps really need to be taken by the senior researcher to obtain supervisory support for research beyond what usually occurs during routine work interactions. In contrast, with the two other types of supervisory views regarding research, an applied researcher needs to take specific actions to obtain supervisory support or, at the minimum, to avoid supervisory interference with research. To understand the rationale for the actions to be described regarding how an applied researcher should go about obtaining support in the latter situations, comment is warranted regarding *why* some executives in human service agencies dislike research.

Although the reasons as to why supervisory or executive personnel in human service agencies view reseach in a negative manner undoubtedly vary across individuals, one relatively common reason seems to be a misunderstanding in terms of what applied research is all about. Directors of human service agencies and upper-level executives generally have essentially no knowledge about, and no experience with, the type of problem-solving research described in this text. Rather, their familiarity with research is related to more basic or theoretical research activities that have no direct bearing on the improvement of human services, and even their familiarity with this type of traditional research is usually minimal. Consequently, given the mission of their agencies to provide human services, they see research as representing something that is unrelated to their job roles and the roles of their agencies. Such individuals also view agency staff involvement in research as something that is likely to interfere with the staff's routine job duties (i.e. because the research with which the staff would be involved has no relation to the mission of the human service agency). In many cases, this view of research among agency executives is rather well founded when considering past attempts of various professionals to conduct non-applied research within the executives' agencies (see Chapter 2 for elaboration).

Given the orientation of many supervisors in human service agencies as just described and their lack of familiarity with problem-solving research, a large part of the process of obtaining supervisory support (or avoiding supervisory interference) for conducting research is to re-educate supervisors regarding the relevance of applied behavioral research. There are essentially two major means of providing such a re-education. One means is to convince the supervisors of the merits of (problem-solving) research by *discussing* the nature and general methodology of this type of research. The second method is to convince the supervisors of the merits of applied research through example; by *conducting* successful research and then taking specific steps to clearly demonstrate how the research undertaking improved some aspect of an agency's service delivery. The later approach has a number of advantages over the former approach, including being more effective and, hence, that is the process to be described here.

Action Steps for Working with Supervisors on Research

Before describing specific steps that can be helpful for a senior researcher in terms of working with supervisors on research, reiteration regarding the type of research that is referred to here is in order. Specifically, the steps to be described really pertain only to *applied, problem-solving research*. Because other types of research do not coincide with the mission of most human service agencies or with routine service activities within such agencies as does the type of applied research stressed here, the reader is cautioned that other steps are warranted for working with agency executives regarding research that does not meet the problem-solving criteria (see, for example, the following section, "Complying With Agency Policy Regarding Research").

When working with supervisors who, at best, appreciate research but do not actively support it and, at worse, overtly discourage research, the first goal of an applied researcher in terms of initiating a research project should not be to obtain the supervisor's support; rather, the goal should be to *avoid* the supervisor's interference and/or disallowance of the project. Basically, if the latter goal is obtained, the senior researcher can then proceed with his/her investigation and, using the action steps to be described, later obtain some actual supervisory support for the research by demonstrating that the project has really aided the agency (and the supervisor). Once a research project has brought about some needed change in the agency, it then becomes easier for the researcher to interact with a supervisor regarding a research undertaking, and the former's goal is no longer to avoid interference by the supervisor but to strengthen the latter's support for research. In this regard, in the preceding chapter it was emphasized that a senior researcher will not be very successful in the long run if active research involvement by his/her *staff* is not developed. In contrast, a senior researcher can be successful without the active involvement and support of his/her *supervisor,* provided that the research coincides with the senior researcher's agency service responsibilities and that the supervisor does not specifically disallow research. However, research endeavors are usually more efficient and pleasant if a supervisor does support a senior researcher's research efforts.

Once a senior researcher has developed an idea for a research project along the lines described in Chapter 2, the first step in working with a supervisor is to inform him/her regarding the general purpose of the research undertaking. The intent should not be to make a detailed proposal regarding the proposed research project but, rather, to describe an existing problem within the human service agency that the senior researcher wants to resolve in a systematic, data-based fashion. The rationale for a systematic, data-based approach can be explained to the supervisor, in that, for example, such an approach allows the senior researcher and other staff to objectively evaluate the extent to which the given problem has been resolved and, if the problem is indeed resolved, to articulate to other persons and/or agencies exactly how the problem was addressed such that they might approach the same type of problem in a similar manner. Generally, if an idea for a research project is presented in this format (provided, of course, that a true agency problem is being addressed), a supervisor is not likely to seriously discourage the senior researcher from proceeding.

An alternative approach for an applied researcher in terms of working with a supervisor is to simply begin addressing a certain agency problem from an applied behavioral format without explicitly informing the supervisor regarding the research-related part of the undertaking. The latter approach is usually effective if, for whatever reason, the senior researcher typically goes about his/her routine job with minimal contact with the supervisor. In such a situation the senior researcher simply does his/her job as usual with the addition of the research activities. The supervisor is likely to be unaware of the research activity, in that he/she is unaware of much of what the senior researcher does as part of the routine work schedule. However, in most cases it is probably more advantageous to inform the supervisor about a proposed research project. By informing the supervisor, he/she will have some knowledge about what is going on and that information can be beneficial for the senior researcher. In particular, if a supervisor subsequently hears about various actions implemented by a senior researcher from other agency staff members, the supervisor generally will react more positively if he/she already has direct knowledge about the endeavor. In this respect, a general organizational rule for an applied researcher to follow (whether pertaining to a research project or a nonresearch job duty) is that, for any serious undertaking, it is usually best to let the supervisor know about the plans prior to taking any action; supervisors typically feel more comfortable knowing firsthand about a major activity going on within their domain of responsibilty relative to finding out indirectly from another source. The amount of information to share with the supervisor about the planned research activity essentially depends on the supervisor's interest, as the more interest he/she shows in the senior researcher's idea, the more detail should be provided by the senior researcher.

Another advantage of a senior researcher sharing an idea for resolving an agency problem in a systematic, data-based fashion (i.e. an applied behavioral research project) with a supervisor is that the process might result in some active support from the supervisor. Depending in part on how much the supervisor shares the senior researcher's concern for the relevance of the problem that is to be addressed, the supervisor might become quite interested in assisting the senior researcher. Although typically the assistance will not be in the form of technical research support because most supervisors have not been trained in research technology, the assistance can be helpful in other ways. The supervisor may, for example, be able to provide extra staff assistance for conducting parts of the project, evoke staff cooperation with the project, or provide resource assistance such as material and equipment funds.

After the supervisor has been informed regarding the senior researcher's idea for an investigation, the next step is for the senior researcher to actually conduct the project. If the supervisor seemed to be somewhat interested in the research idea when the senior researcher initially shared the idea with the supervisor, then the senior researcher should periodically update the supervisor regarding the status of the project. As with the initial idea-sharing process with the supervisor, the degree of elaboration provided by the senior researcher to the supervisor should be based on the amount of interest in the project expressed by the supervisor during the update meetings. On the other hand, if the supervisor did not express very much interest in the research during the initial interaction about the research idea, then the senior researcher should omit the periodic updates and proceed to the third action step.

The third action step for working with a supervisor occurs when the research project has been completed and the paper describing the investigation is being written. At that point, the results of the project in terms of resolution of the agency problem should be shared with the supervisor. Additionally, formal acknowledgment of the agency's and the supervisor's support of the research in terms of allowing the investigation to occur should be provided within the paper. The purpose of acknowledging the agency and supervisor in this manner is severalfold. First, such acknowledgment is professionally appropriate and deserving. In short, the supervisor did allow the work to occur even if he/she may not have actively supported the research, and the given investigation could not have occurred without the cooperation of the agency. Second, most supervisors will appreciate the acknowledgment, and such appreciation can enhance the senior reseacher's future research endeavors by making the supervisor more receptive to applied research. The appreciation may exist on a somewhat personal level by the supervisor, in that he/she sincerely appreciates the senior researcher recognizing the important role that the supervisor played in supporting the research. Additionally, even though many supervisors are not particularly interested in applied research per se, they are appreciative when a component of their agency's service provision has been improved. Relatedly, many supervisors will be appreciative of the external recognition (i.e. from other agencies and professionals) their agency receives when a successful problem-solving research project that was conducted in their agency is published as a journal article.

Avoiding Self-Induced Procrastination in Doing Research: A Caution Against Over-Talking Research

In considering the process just described in terms of a senior researcher interacting with a supervisor about a research idea, a word of caution is in order. Actually, the caution pertains not only to interactions with a supervisor but in essence to interactions that an applied researcher has with anyone. The concern is due to the situation that often arises in human service agencies in which prospective researchers spend more time *talking* about research than actually *conducting* research. This situation develops for a couple of reasons. First, doing research requires a considerable amount of hard work relative to talking about research. Although talking about research usually reflects sincere intentions on the part of a prospective researcher in regard to wanting to conduct a research project, people nevertheless tend to gravitate to less effortful tasks (in this case, talking versus doing). Second, prospective researchers can receive considerable recognition from research-interested peers for talking about research. In such a situation, a researcher often can receive positive feedback for describing an innovative research topic, for example, or for developing a seemingly ingenius experimental design for investigating a given topic. The positive attention and recognition from peers frequently encourage the prospective researcher to continue engaging in discussions about his/her research plans, which in turn competes with the senior researcher's time and energy for actually conducting the research project. Relatedly, many human service agencies are rather notorious for operating on a meeting or committee basis which tends to foster frequent discussions about services among agency staff members but not necessarily any action in terms of someone assuming the responsibility of actually doing something about improving services. This type of agency-operating focus can easily carry over to research issues. Consequently, an applied researcher needs to guard against the *talking-but-not-doing trap*. Generally, if a senior researcher finds that he/she has been talking about a potential research project frequently for several weeks but has not begun the project by at least collecting initial baseline data, then the senior researcher should terminate such discussions until the project has been initiated.

A related problem that stems from a senior researcher falling into the talking-but-not-doing trap is the impact the process has on prospective research colleagues. If an applied researcher has been successful in involving some of the agency's most competent staff in the planning stages of a research project, then those staff will become disillusioned with the lack of progress. As discussed earlier in Chapter 3, a senior researcher should strive to involve an agency's most competent staff as collaborators on a research project. However, those types of staff persons are usually "doers" and not "talkers" and will quickly become tired of hearing the senior researcher's discussions without any corresponding action. Such staff persons will subsequently lose interest in collaborating with the senior researcher relative to doing something more productive during their job routine. Concern for staff losing interest in a research project is particularly important during the planning stages of an investigation. In essence, for staff (including senior researchers) who are seriously interested in seeing action occur to improve some aspect of a human service agency's operation, the planning stage of an applied research undertaking is usually the most frustrating part of the project. Planning a good applied study requires a considerable amount of time and thought, as well as piloting and repeatedly refining various data-collection systems and other procedural components. The planning activities invariably cause a rather lengthy delay between the time a problem-solving research idea is conceived and when the actual implementation of the intervention designed to resolve the problem takes place. If the delay in implementing the intervention becomes too lengthy, research staff can become frustrated relatively easily. Consequently, the senior researcher needs to be very cautious to not extend the delay needlessly because of "over-talking" the intended project.

Complying With Agency Policy Regarding Research

An important aspect in conducting research in a human service agency that relates to developing supervisory support is to abide by official agency policies regarding research activity. Most human service agencies, and essentially all such agencies that receive federal financial support, have explicit policies regarding guidelines for conducting research. The policies specify such things as the approval process that must be followed prior to initiating an investigation in order to protect the interest of the participating clients, as well as the format for presenting results of the project in order to protect confidentiality of participants. It is incumbent upon an applied researcher to become thoroughly familiar with these types of policies. In this regard, compliance with research policies by a senior researcher is really not a negotiable issue; it simply must occur to protect the welfare of everyone involved in the research, including the senior researcher. However, at times agency research policies do not pertain to applied, problem-solving investigations. Research policies historically have been developed using a definition of research based on traditional, academically related experimentation. If the problem-solving format for conducting applied research as discussed in Chapters 1 and 2 is followed, then the resulting research activities are likely to be formally excluded from falling within the guidelines of typical research policies. In one sense, problem-solving research should be excluded from formal research guidelines, because this type of research represents an activity that probably should occur within the auspices of a human service agency on a regular basis (i.e. attempting to improve some aspect of an agency's service delivery). The only difference is that the problem-solving research approach must be more systematic and data based than usual agency attempts to solve a given problem.

In cases where applied, problem-solving research is excluded from complying with agency research policies, an advantage exists for the senior researcher. The advantage is that, often, following official approval mechanisms for conducting research that exist in standard research policies can be a time-consuming, bureaucratically ladened process. Such a process can seriously delay the implementation of a research project.

In order to determine if his/her prospective research project is exempt from complying with agency research guidelines, a senior researcher must, of course, be knowledgable about an agency's research policy. In some cases, even *if* a potential project is excluded from guidelines imposed by a research policy, an applied researcher should take the additional steps to meet the policy guidelines. In particular, if other researchers within the agency have been criticized in the past for not complying with the research policy, a senior researcher should overtly attempt to operate within the policy guidelines. At times, researchers have created a negative impression on staff in human service agencies because the staff were aware that the researchers operated in apparent disregard for established agency policy. Where this situation has occurred, an applied researcher should comply with a research policy, even if on a voluntary basis, to avoid creating a negative impact on staff and, relatedly, to avoid fostering potential staff resistance to his/her particular research undertaking. (See Chapter 2 for elaboration on how staff resistance to research in human services is generated.)

Obtaining External Agency Support

(Mis)Use of Grant Resources

One of the most popular means of attempting to secure assistance in conducting research within a human service agency is to seek resources through an external grant. Numerous types of grant assistance are available from private and governmental agencies that can be useful to an applied researcher in obtaining additional resources for research purposes. However, although grant assistance can be quite helpful, using grant support for research purposes also can have some serious disadvantages. In particular, there are several rather common misuses of grant resources that prospective senior researchers should strive to *avoid*. As a point of clarification, the reference to "misuse" is somewhat different from how the term is often referred to, in that it does not mean any illegal or unethical use of grant monies. Rather, as referred to here, "misuse" means a disadvantageous reliance on grant resources such that a senior researcher's research productivity is hindered relative to not using grant assistance for research purposes.

The most serious problem that arises when an applied researcher looks toward grant resources for assistance in conducting research is that an over-reliance on the grant support develops. To illustrate, a frequent sequence of events that occurs in human service agencies is that a senior researcher wants to conduct research and realizes that extra manpower is needed. An application for grant support is then completed and submitted to a funding agency, the senior researcher waits at least several months for a response from the funding source, and the funding agency subsequently responds and rejects the application. Consequently, the research project is never initiated. In this sequence of events, the senior researcher has become overly reliant on (potential) grant assistance as a means of conducting research and, hence, when the grant support falls through then so does the research project.

An argument could be made that if the scenario just described is altered in terms of the funding agency's decision such that the senior researcher does receive the grant support, then the researcher can proceed with the research project and is actually better able to conduct the investigation than if he/she had not sought extra assistance from a grant. In some ways this latter point of view is accurate, because the extra manpower obtained through grant funding can be quite helpful. However, in the long run, there are still some serious disadvantages that suggest that grant funds should not be sought very often. For one thing, completing grant applications is usually a very time-consuming process; such time could be spent actually initiating a research project by utilizing support indigenous to the senior researcher's human service agency (Chap. 3). Relatedly, it often takes an extended period of time for a funding agency to respond to a grant request—time that, again, could be spent by a senior researcher actually conducting research instead of waiting for a response.

Another major disadvantage of relying on external grant support for research assistance is highlighted in the scenario just described: grant requests are not always fulfilled. Actually, most grant requests are probably denied. Funding sources for research-related grants are finite and, hence, can only be used to fund a sample of prospective projects. Further, there is usually considerable competition for the grant money that is available. Many times, a senior researcher is not in a situation to functionally compete with other agencies (and particularly with universities), for available grant monies. To illustrate, a senior researcher typically has to search for potential funding sources and to prepare a grant application totally on his/her own. In contrast, in many universities there are specified staff and systems available to help prospective researchers know immediately when and where certain grant monies are available as well as to help complete the application and solicit appropriate support for the application from influential persons. Additionally, the senior researcher often has to compete with university programs and personnel who have long-standing, successful track records with certain funding agencies and who may have rather personal working relations with grant agencies. In short, although some senior researchers in applied settings certainly have been successful in obtaining grant support for research, generally most applied researchers in human service agencies are not able to successfully compete with university programs.

A final disadvantage of the use of grant support for conducting applied research is that such support is always temporary. If a given research project is dependent on grant support for existence, when the grant support ends the project usually is terminated, also. In this regard, grants are by nature funded on a time-limited basis, and research projects may or may not be appropriately completed when the time frame for the grant has expired.

Because of the problems with reliance on grant support, a senior researcher should be quite careful in seeking grant funds. Probably, the best guideline is to *not use* grants as a means of conducting research. However, due in part to the success some applied researchers have had in obtaining grant support for research purposes, there would undoubtedly be disagreement with such a stringent recommendation. A less controversial guideline would be to use grant support only for supplemental assistance for a research project in contrast to heavily relying on the support. In this manner, a research project is basically established without grant support and then, if such support becomes available, it is used to supplement what is already established. For example, if grant support becomes available through personnel monies, the funding could be used to hire additional observers for data-collection purposes. The observers could relieve (but not replace) staff observers and lessen the latter's work load on the research project. When used in this fashion, if the grant funding expires, the research project can continue without much difficulty because the staff observers can resume their previous responsibilities that were temporarily (and partially) fulfilled by grant-funded observers.

A second guideline that can be helpful to an applied researcher in regard to grant support is to seek grants that are relatively non-competitive. Of course, other things being equal, the fewer agencies that a senior researcher has to compete with for grant funds, the more likely it is that the senior researcher's grant will be funded. Grants that are restricted by geographic regions and/or type of agencies that are eligible to receive the grant monies generally are not excessively competitive. Hence, a senior researcher is more likely to have success with a potential grant that is available only within his/her state and available only to his/her specific type of human service agency than with a grant that is available on a national level to many types of university and non-university agencies. Examples of the former types of grants are those sponsored by private foundations with a within-state focus and those provided by a state government office that is within the same governmental unit or department as the senior researcher's own human service agency.

A third guideline for enhancing the successful use of grant support is for the senior researcher to seek only grants that require a relatively small amount of time to prepare the grant application. By quickly screening different grant application forms, an applied researcher can usually determine approximately how much time and effort will be required to seek a given grant based on the amount (and complexity) of the information requested within the application. The less time that is required to complete an application, then the less time is lost if the grant is not funded and, more importantly, the more time can be devoted to actually working on a research project. Generally, the types of grants described earlier that are relatively less competitive are also the types of grants that are less time consuming to seek.

A final guideline in regard to grant utilization is to focus on relatively small grants, grants that typically provide between $5,000 and $50,000. Relative to grants that involve hundreds of thousands of dollars, smaller grants usually have the advantages just discussed of being less competitive and less time consuming to seek. Of course, smaller grants provide fewer resources than larger grants and, consequently, the latter often appear more attractive to applied researchers. Nevertheless, the development and maintenance of an applied research program within a human service agency is more likely to succeed over the long run with the assistance of small grants than large grants, at least if any grant assistance is used. By the nature of the large number of external personnel and resources employed through large grants, it is usually very difficult to synthesize the grant-funded research activities into the routine operation of a human service agency and to use the grant resources in a supplemental manner as discussed earlier. Rather, the research is usually conducted by the numerous (non-agency) grant personnel independent from the agency's daily operation. Consequently, when the grant expires and the grant personnel are no longer available, the research is terminated, whether completed or not. Further, because agency staff are not involved in conducting the grant-funded research, they do not learn any research skills that they normally would acquire by being integrally involved in research conducted by a senior researcher in the agency (Chap. 3). As a result, the grant-funded research does little if anything to foster future research involvement by agency staff. These types of problems with the use of large grants (and numerous grant-funded personnel) for research support are in many ways analogous to the problems frequently associated with non-agency personnel such as university faculty conducting research in human service settings (Chap. 2).

Use of Student Assistance

For a number of human service agencies, a good source of external support for research is college and university student assistance. Of course, an agency must be located within a community that has a college or university close by if the agency is to have regular access to student assistance. Fortunately, in this regard, because of the hundreds of state and privately supported colleges and universities throughout the United

States, as well as the hundreds of community colleges, many human service agencies are quite close to a potential source of student assistance (cf. Lagomarcino, et al., 1986).

Probably the most advantageous involvement of students in terms of research support for a senior researcher is collaboration on student theses and dissertations. In many cases graduate students are looking for applied settings in which to conduct their master's thesis or doctoral dissertation research, and the senior researcher's human service agency may represent such a setting. However, student involvement in research in human service settings is a process that requires some careful planning and action steps on the part of the senior researcher if the involvement is to be successful for the senior researcher (as well as his/her agency) and the student. This chapter section presents suggested strategies for increasing the likelihood of successful student-senior researcher collaboration along with some typical problems that occur if the involvement is not well coordinated.

The first issue that warrants attention in regard to student involvement in reseach in human service settings is the topic of the student's research. In essence, the topic must meet the same applied problemsolving characteristics (Chap. 1 and 2) as any of the other research undertakings of the senior researcher, if the student's research is to be effectively coordinated within the operation of a human service agency. The senior researcher must determine whether or not the student's proposed research topic meets these criteria; if the criteria are not met, the senior researcher should advise the student that the latter's research ideas either need to be altered or that another site for the research should be located. In many situations, however, the topic of the research will not be an issue in terms of not representing a relevant problem-solving idea, because the student will not be exactly sure what his/her thesis or dissertation topic will be. In such a situation, the senior researcher can assist the student by sharing ideas from the problem list (Chap. 2) from which the student can select a topic of interest to him/herself as well as a topic of benefit to the senior researcher's agency. The latter type of process has resulted in a number of successful research endeavors that addressed relevant problem areas within human service agencies. For example, Lou Burgio's doctoral dissertation at the University of Notre Dame resulted in the development of an innovative and effective program for assisting paraprofessional staff in an institution to conduct therapeutic interactions with profoundly mentally retarded persons (Burgio, Whitman & Reid, 1984).

A major consideration in the selection of an appropriate topic of research for a student, as well as in the other aspects of conducting a study, is the existence of a cooperative working arrangement between not only the student and the senior researcher but also between the student's university mentor and the senior researcher. In essence the primary issue in such an arrangement is who is in control of the direction and implementation of the research: the student, the student's university adviser, or the senior researcher? From the point of view of a successful applied research project within the confines of a human service agency, the ultimate decision maker (or at least the ability to have veto power) must be the senior researcher. If the senior researcher does not have the authority to make final decisions (or to veto) in regard to the design and implementation of the investigation, then the same problems as described in Chapter 2 that occur with university-based faculty conducting research in human service settings are likely to occur with the student's thesis or dissertation research.

Generally, the most effective means of establishing the appropriate decision-making process as just described is for the senior researcher to specifically present the operating guidelines to the student and his/her university adviser prior to initiation of any aspect of the student's research. If the guidelines are presented in this manner, all parties can become aware of how things will operate, and if agreement cannot be reached, a decision can be made at that point that it would be in the best interest of all parties not to conduct the research in the senior researcher's agency. Unfortunately such arrangements often are not established prior to a student initiating a study, with the result that the investigation never becomes successful and/or ill will develops between the university-based individuals and the senior researcher or other agency staff. However, if the process just described can be established satisfactorily, then the senior researcher can approach the student's collaboration on a research project in the same manner as he/she approaches research with other agency personnel as described intermittently throughout this text. In this regard, one of the points of agreement that should be established prior to the student initiating the research is that if agency personnel work closely with the student and/or senior researcher on the project (which is usually required if the study is to be truly successful within the agency), then those agency personnel should be co-authors of the article that (hopefully) results from the study. The rationale for including agency staff as co-authors with the university-based individuals is the same as that for involving agency staff as co-authors with the senior researcher (Chap. 7).

In addition to working as a co-experimenter with a senior researcher on a thesis or dissertation, students can also represent a source of external agency support for research by fulfilling a role that is less integral on a given research project. If a college or university is located close to a human service agency, often a practicum or internship arrangement can be established. In such situations, part of the working agreement with the university can be that the student spend part of his/her practicum or internship time helping with a research project. The student help in this regard (e.g. as a data collector) should be treated in essentially the same supplemental manner as temporary grant support (as described earlier in this chapter) in order to ensure that the most effective type of assistance is provided by the student.

Using Agency Personnel Systems to Obtain Extra Assistance for Research

The use of grant resources and student involvement as just discussed represents probably the best known approach for obtaining external agency support for research. Another approach that, in many cases, is more readily available to an applied researcher, although it is often overlooked, is the use of personnel systems existing within human service agencies. Most, if not all, human service agencies have an official process for employing staff, and that process can be used periodically to employ temporary personnel to assist with a research project without interfering with the routine utilization of agency staff positions. To frequently utilize personnel systems in this manner, two criteria generally must be met. First, a senior researcher must have a very thorough understanding of the intricacies of his/her agency's personnel rules and regulations, with particular knowledge regarding staff hiring practices. Second, the senior researcher must be in an authoritative position within an agency (Chap. 3) in order to have the necessary control to consistently utilize the personnel system advantageously for applied research purposes.

An example of how an agency's personnel system can be used to acquire research assistance is represented when there is staff turnover within an agency. Staff persons invariably come and go within agencies which creates temporary position vacancies until new staff are employed. In such cases, if a senior researcher is knowledgeable regarding personnel practices for expeditiously hiring temporary staff, the vacancies created by staff turnover can be used to employ persons to help with a research project (e.g. as a data collector) until the agency has found a permanent replacement for the parted staff member. Employing temporary research help in this manner can be accomplished without really detracting from other potential agency services, because, often, temporary vacancies created by staff turnover are not utilized by the agency for anything; the positions simply remain vacant until new (permanent) staff members are employed.

Another example of how a personnel system can be used advantageously by a senior researcher to obtain temporary help for a research project is represented by the somewhat creative utilization of part-time staff positions. Sometimes, a given staff member may be approved by an agency's management to change from full-time employment to part-time. For example, a staff member may wish to return from maternity leave on a part-time basis only. In many agencies, what results in this type of situation is a staff position that has been funded on a full-time basis but subsequently utilizes only part of the funding such that extra salary monies are available. Again, if a senior researcher is knowledgeable regarding personnel employment rules and regulations, he/she can use those "extra" salary monies to employ part-time research help. As with the temporary use of vacant staff positions just described, often the use of monies resulting from a newly developed part-time arrangement of a staff position are not normally used by the agency for other purposes. Hence, the senior researcher's use of the monies for research assistance does not functionally detract from other agency services.

A concern that arises at times with the use of staff positions as just described is that personnel policies may be broken because a designated staff position is being used for something other than what the official job description for the position specifies—in this case, research. The unused part of a part-time physical therapist position, for example, might be used temporarily as a data collector as part of a research project. Potential problems with using staff positions for purposes other than what is specified in the job description usually can be circumvented if the senior researcher has a thorough knowledge regarding personnel rules and regulations as just stressed. To illustrate, many personnel systems in government-based agencies include a process whereby positions can be used "out of class" (i.e. for duties other than the specified job description) for a temporary period of time, such as for three to six months pending appropriate management approval. If an applied researcher is knowledgeable about "out of class" provisions and related personnel operating procedures, he/she can use the personnel system quite advantageously for research-assistance purposes. Additional methods of dealing with job-description issues in regard to research were noted in Chapter 3.

In essence, with the appropriate knowledge and authority, a senior researcher frequently has a rather large pool of potential means of employing staff for research assistance within his/her own agency. Sometimes, agency personnel offices can be very helpful in determining means of employing temporary research staff, with the degree of help provided depending in large part on the existence of a good working relationship between the senior researcher and the staff in the personnel office. However, an applied researcher would nevertheless be wise in the long run to not rely solely on the personnel staff in this regard. Rather, a senior researcher should have sufficient knowledge to be able to provide his/her own creative ideas on how to (appropriately) use personnel systems for research purposes.

REFERENCES

Burgio, L. D., Whitman, T. L., & Reid, D. H. (1983). A participative management approach for improving direct-care staff performance in an institutional setting. *Journal of Applied Behavior Analysis, 16,* 37-53.

Dunst, C. J. (1985). Editor's introduction. *Analysis and Intervention in Developmental Disabilities, 5,* 1-5.

Favell, J. E., McGimsey, J. F., & Schell, R. M. (1982). Treatment of self-injury by providing alternate sensory activities. *Analysis and Intervention in Developmental Disabilities, 2,* 83-104.

Green, C. W., Canipe, V. S., Way, P. J., & Reid, D. H. (1986). Improving the functional utility and effectiveness of classroom services for students with profound multiple handicaps. *Journal of the Association for Persons with Severe Handicaps, 11,* 162-170.

Lagomarcino, A., Reid, D. H., Phillips, J. F., & Wilson, P. G. (1986). Increasing volunteering at a residential facility: An experimental evaluation of a volunteer assistance program. *Behavioral Residential Treatment, 1,* 125-136.

Realon, R. E., Favell, J. E., Stirewalt, S. C., & Phillips, J. F. (1986). Teaching severely handicapped persons to provide leisure activities to peers. *Analysis and Intervention in Developmental Disabilities, 6,* 203-219.

Schepis, M. M., Reid, D. H., & Fitzgerald, J. D. (1987). Group instruction with profoundly retarded persons: Acquisition, generalization and maintenance of a remunerative work skill. *Journal of Applied Behavior Analysis,* in press.

Chapter 5

CHARACTERISTICS OF TECHNICAL RESEARCH PROCEDURES MOST AMENABLE TO APPLIED SETTINGS

IN CHAPTER 1 the importance of applied behavior analysis was noted in terms of fostering applied research undertakings in human service settings. In essence, the development and dissemination of applied behavioral research technologies beginning in the early 1960s have resulted in an unprecedented growth in the amount of reseach conducted in human service agencies. The reasons why applied behavior analysis has had such a stimulating effect on human services research relative to more traditional approaches to research (e.g. group comparisons, statistical estimations) (see Barlow & Herson, 1984) are severalfold. Perhaps, most importantly, applied behavior analysis focuses on resolving problems of immediate social relevance — problems like those that human service agencies face on a regular basis. In contrast, more traditional research often addresses issues of a theoretical nature that have only an indirect relationship (if any relationship) to socially relevant problems.

In addition to a focus on issues of social significance, behavior analysis research methodology facilitates the conducting of research in human service settings because of its responsive experimental-design features. That is, an underlying premise of applied behavior analysis research is that an experimental design should be selected and/or modified within an investigation to suit the problem that is being addressed. In more traditional research often the reverse is true; the research question being addressed has to be altered to fit within the confines of a given experimental design. Elaboration on how an experimental design can be molded around a problem-solving task as part of an applied behavior analysis investigation in a human service agency will be provided later in this chapter.

Another feature of applied behavior analysis that facilitates research in human service settings is its focus on the individual. More specifically, a primary concern in behavior analysis research projects from both an experimental-control and social-significance standpoint is the effect of the experimental intervention on individual participants. In contrast, more traditional research focuses on the effect on large groups of participants, with a relative lack of attention directed to the impact on any given individual within the group. The advantages and disadvantages of the focus on the individual versus the group in terms of appropriate research methodology have been discussed thoroughly elsewhere (Barlow & Herson, 1984) and such discussion is really not that relevant here. What is relevant for purposes of discussion here is that, due in large part to the focus on individual participants, good applied behavior analysis research can be conducted with a small number of participants (often five or less). From a practicality standpoint, it is frequently easier to conduct an applied research project in a human service setting with four or five experimental participants, for example, than with several dozens of participants (the latter number is rather common in more traditional research). Of course, the ultimate number of participants in a particular study should be determined by the nature of the problem that is being addressed; as many participants should be included as necessary to solve the problem. Nevertheless, in cases where one of an agency's problems of concern can be addressed satisfactorily by including a relatively small number of individuals as experimental participants, applied behavior analysis research methodology can be much more easily used than traditional, group-oriented approaches to research.

The characteristics of applied behavior analysis just noted represent only a sample of the features of this approach to research that facilitate its employment within human service settings. In this regard, since the initial development of applied behavior analysis, the variety and number of experimental strategies that have become available for use in applied settings has expanded rather tremendously, which further facilitates the task of the applied researcher in terms of the ability to conduct research in human service agencies. However, some experimental strategies are better suited than others in regard to the ease with which they allow for research to be successfully conducted in applied settings. Some experimental strategies are generally better than others, because, for example, they require less work on the part of the experimenters. Some procedures are better than others because they are less likely to have things go wrong during a study as a result of the varied non-research activities ongoing within human service agencies. Hence, a senior researcher must be able to choose those specific experimental strategies that are most amenable to his/her research topic and setting in order to maximize the probability of conducting a successful project. This chapter discusses guidelines for selecting research strategies that are best suited for conducting successful research within the confines of typical human service settings.

Selecting a Workable Research Topic

Generally, the first concern in selecting research strategies that are amenable to the operations of a human service agency is to select a research topic that is *workable*. A workable topic is one that, on a relative basis, has a high probability of success in terms of: (a) being able to be addressed on a day-to-day basis by the senior researcher and his/her colleagues *in conjunction with* other work responsibilities within the human service agency; and (b) having a good likelihood of actually solving the agency problem that is being addressed. A number of features determine whether the work involved in conducting a research project can actually be performed on a daily basis and whether the targeted problem has a reasonable chance of being resolved. However, before elaborating on these characteristics of a workable research topic, several other important parameters of a research topic that have been discussed in previous chapters warrant review. In essence, three criteria for selecting a research topic must be met prior to being concerned about whether the topic is workable in the fashion just noted. First, the topic must focus on an important problem within the agency; the research must be problem solving in nature (see Chapter 1 for elaboration). Second, the topic must be one that, when resolved, will make a contribution to the professional research literature (Chap. 2). Third, the topic should be one that is selected with the active involvement of the senior researcher's staff collaborators on the research project (Chap. 3). For purposes of discussion here, it will be assumed that each of these three criteria are adhered to in selecting a topic of research. The remainder of this chapter section discusses areas that should be attended to if a research topic that has the three characteristics just noted is also to be *workable*.

Avoiding Comparison Investigations

One very useful type of research, in terms of advancing human service provision, is that which compares two or more methods of resolving a given human service problem. Generally, this type of research occurs after a number of investigations have been published in which different experimental interventions across the various investigations have been demonstrated to be successful at resolving the same type of problem. A comparison investigation is then conducted to see which of the interventions is *most* effective in resolving the problem. For example, a number of procedures for reducing self-injurious behavior of profoundly mentally retarded persons have been evaluated in different investigations. Dorsey et al. (1982) subsequently compared several of these procedures, such as various punishment methods and protective equipment strategies, in one single investigation in an attempt to determine the *relative* efficacy of each procedure.

Although comparison investigations of the type just noted can contribute highly useful information for improving human service delivery systems, these types of studies are very difficult to conduct effectively in typical human service settings. Consequently, senior researchers are encouraged to avoid this type of research if they want to maximize their chances of completing successful research projects. The difficulty involved in conducting comparison research in human service agencies, and the subsequent recommendation for applied researchers to avoid this type of research, are due to several factors. One such factor is that behavior analysis research designs generally are not as well suited for comparison investigations relative to more traditional, group-oriented research designs. Essentially, it is difficult to establish appropriate experimental controls in comparison research with behavior analysis research designs. A discussion of the technical reasons why experimental control is difficult to establish with behavior analysis designs in comparison research is provided elsewhere (Kazdin, 1982). Suffice it to say here that it is much easier, from an experimental design standpoint, to conduct an applied research project in a human service setting that does *not* involve comparing two or more problem-solving interventions.

The difficulties in using behavior analysis research designs to conduct comparison research actually exist in any settings in which research is conducted, not just human service settings. However, there are also difficulties with comparison research that are specific to human service settings that further cause this type of research to be problematic. In particular, comparison research requires that basically all experimental procedures for all participants in a research project be identical except for the specific interventions that are to be compared. For example, if two training strategies are being compared for relative effectiveness in teaching vocational skills to mentally retarded persons, then the experimental participants should receive the same exposure to each training strategy (e.g. participate in the same number of training sessions with each strategy over equivalent time periods) such that one strategy will not appear superior because the participants simply were exposed to it more than the other strategy. In most human service agencies, precise involvement of clients in training programs is difficult to control, much less *equate* across different training programs for research purposes. Training sessions for a client may be delayed or cancelled because the staff trainer is sick for a week, because the client participated in a special event such as a birthday party, because a staff observer is pulled away from a research project temporarily because of a competing job responsibility in the agency, etc. In these types of situations, if a comparison study is being conducted, then the altered training schedule for one client with one of the targeted training strategies must be controlled for by altering the training schedule of that same client with the other training strategy and/or with other clients' training schedules. In short, there are many events — both planned and unplanned — that a senior researcher must remain aware of and control for in order to conduct good comparison research. Such a task not only increases a senior researcher's work load in conducting a study, it also increases the likelihood that something will go wrong experimentally due to the numerous activities that occur in human service settings that the senior research cannot control.

The recommendation for a senior researcher to avoid comparison research in human service agencies does not mean that such research cannot be accomplished. As indicated in the example cited earlier (and there are numerous other examples), successful comparison research has been conducted in human service settings on a variety of important topics. All things considered, however, a senior researcher is less likely to be successful at comparison research than at applied research that does not involve comparisons of two or more experimental interventions.

Selecting Topics That Directly Relate to Job Responsibilities in a Human Service Setting

As discussed in Chapter 3, a senior researcher and his/her research colleagues can be employed in a variety of different job roles in a human service agency. When trying to select a workable research topic, it is most advantageous to choose a topic that most clearly and directly relates to the job responsibilities of the role that the senior researcher or one of his/her colleagues fulfills. In this manner, involvement in the research activity can be more easily synthesized into the senior researcher's (or his/her colleague's) daily job routine than if the research topic focuses on an agency problem that does not directly fall within the senior researcher's job domain. As discussed in Chapter 2, by synthesizing an applied research undertaking into the daily job routine, the research work load of an applied researcher is reduced considerably. In addition, it is less likely that a senior researcher will neglect his/her routine job duties within the agency because of the research involvement if the research addresses a problem that is clearly within the senior researcher's job responsibility.

In most situations, a senior researcher will have an array of important problems within his/her agency service responsibility from which to select a research topic (see Chapter 2 for elaboration). Indeed, the human services represent a considerably less-than-perfect system, and systematic, data-based attempts to improve an aspect of that system to bring it to a level that is closer to perfection represent solid topics for applied research. However, despite the rather large pool of potential research topics, what happens relatively frequently is that an applied researcher attempts to address an agency problem that is *not* under his/her own direct area of responsibility within the agency. Exactly why this situation occurs is unclear. Perhaps, it is because it is sometimes easier or less threatening to highlight problems in someone else's area of responsibility than in one's own area. Regardless, the result of working on research topics that do not fall within a senior researcher's job responsibility is that the senior researcher decreases his/her chances of completing a successful research project. In particular, by working (research-wise) in an area outside of his/her own service responsibility, it is likely that the applied researcher will not have sufficient control of the necessary staff and other agency resources to adequately address the problem; the resources are under the control of whomever is directly responsible for that area of the agency's service delivery. In addition, because the researcher does not routinely work in that specific area within the agency, he/she is not likely to have a very thorough understanding of the problematic situation; consequently, the probability of satisfactorily resolving the problem is decreased. By stepping beyond a given area of authority, a senior researcher also frequently upsets staff members who *do* have the responsibility of working in the particular area by interfering with the latter's work. Such a situation occurs because many staff simply are not very responsive to researchers who are not involved in the staff's routine area of service responsibility, attempting to redirect the staff's work operation because of problems that the researchers have highlighted.

A common example of the problems that occur when an applied researcher attempts to conduct research outside of his/her area of agency work responsibility is represened by research projects that have been frequently attempted in residential facilities for the mentally retarded and mentally ill. A common problem in these settings is a lack of active treatment provision within the living units in which the clientele of the institutions reside (e.g. wards, residential cottages). Many agency staff persons who are not directly responsible for the living unit operations have attempted to improve the treatment provision through applied research undertakings. Psychologists, for example, who usually have consultative and not direct supervisory roles in regard to living unit operations, have attempted numerous applied research projects aimed at increasing active treatment by implementing a variety of staff management systems. What frequently happens is that the psychologist has to convince the supervisors of the living unit that he/she has a solution to the problem and then solicit the supervisors' (rather formidable) efforts to implement the proposed system. Unfortunately, because the psychologist has a relatively restricted understanding of the problem due to the fact that he/she is not intimately involved in the work that is necessary on a day-to-day basis to manage a living unit, the proposed management system usually only addresses a small part of the living unit's problem. Further, in order for the living unit supervisors to implement the psychologist's proposed management system, they generally have to discontinue some portion of their ongoing work activities which in turn causes more problems within the living unit. As a result of this process, the psychologist's management system (and applied research project) usually causes resentment among the supervisors (and often their supervisees) and the research project fails rather miserably (a failure that the author of this text has experienced firsthand as a practicing psychologist). Similarly, the research project, if initially effective, often ends up providing only a temporary solution to the living-unit problem; a solution that continues only as long as the psychologist is conducting his/her formal research project. A much more effective means of conducting a research project to improve active treatment in residential living units is for the research to be conducted by the *actual living-unit supervisor(s)* or by someone who has supervisory responsibility over the living-unit supervisor. (See Chapter 3 regarding a researcher fulfilling an authoritative/supervisory role within a human service agency.)

The example just provided was meant to demonstrate how a senior researcher can inadvertently decrease the probability of conducting a successful research project by addressing an agency problem that is not within his/her area of direct responsibility. However, the example also reflects a general topic of research in terms of *improving staff performance* that can be a very productive undertaking for a senior researcher if a different operational approach is taken. If an applied researcher is in an authoritative type of position in a human service agency, then often he/she *is* responsible for supervising a number of agency staff persons through an organizational chain of command. Hence, a topic of research that *is* directly within the senior researcher's area of responsibility is how to improve the performance of staff that fall under the senior researcher organizationally. Of course, this potential topic of research exists only if there are problems with staff performance. Nevertheless, there frequently are problems with staff performance in many human service settings (as well as other types of settings) that could represent viable topics for applied, problem-solving research. Actually, staff management research has been targeted by applied researchers in authoritative and supervisory roles in a number of human service settings, focusing on resolving such diverse problem areas as insufficient staff-client interactions in state institutions (Burg, Reid, & Lattimore, 1979; Montegar, et al., 1977), inefficient meeting interactions (Hutchison, Jarman, & Bailey, 1980), staff absenteeism (Shoemaker & Reid, 1980), inadequate health care provision (Iwata et al., 1976) and ineffective staff training practices (van den Pol, Reid, & Fuqua, 1983). However, the research to date has really only scratched the surface in terms of what needs to be done in regard to developing effective and durable staff management systems in the human services (Reid & Whitman, 1983).

Although research on staff performance can be a productive research topic for an applied researcher who is employed in an authoritative position as just indicated, a word of caution is in order when considering this type of applied research. Staff management research needs to be conducted with a sincere interest in, and awareness of, the concerns and dignity of the staff persons who function as research participants. Due in large part to a lack of information among staff regarding the purpose of applied behavioral research relative to more traditional, non-applied basic experimentation, staff persons are often somewhat resentful of being "subjects" in an investigation. The resentment frequently occurs when: (a) staff do not know why their performance is being systematically monitored, which is usually a necesssary component in behavioral staff management research; and/or (b) staff have inaccurate information about why their performance is being monitored; and/or (c) staff find out after the fact that their performance has been monitored for purposes of a research project.

Probably, the best means of avoiding potential staff resentment regarding their participation in a research project is to openly discuss the purpose of the project *prior* to initiating the investigation. Even if all aspects of a given study may not be able to be shared with the staff initially in order to protect the integrity of the experimental design (i.e. to protect any type of staff or supervisor bias from affecting the research outcome), staff should at least be informed of the general purpose of the undertaking. If the focus of the research is truly addressing an important topic, such as improving a designated component of client service delivery, often staff will understand and/or accept the rationale for conducting a research project as a means of making necessary improvements. Nevertheless, even when these steps are taken by a senior researcher there can inadvertently be some resentment among staff. Such resentment may be due for example, to unpleasant experiences staff have had with research in the past, miscommunication through the organizational chain of command regarding the purpose of the research project, or an unpleasant manner in which a supervisor carries out part of the research procedures. Serious resentment among staff regarding their participation in research is generally easy for the senior researcher to detect if he/she is integrally involved in conducting the research. When serious resentment does develop, the senior researcher would be wise to direct his/her research efforts to another topic and forego staff management research. Creating dissatisfaction among an agency's staff members by involving them in research as unwilling experimental participants not only results in an unpleasant work environment for staff (as well as an agency's clients and the senior researcher), but it also can cause future problems for an applied researcher in terms of staff resistance to other research projects.

Selecting Experimental Designs that Facilitate the Research Task

In the introductory comments to this chapter, an advantage of applied behavior analysis research technology was noted in regard to the experimental designs used in this type of research. Specifically, applied behavioral research designs are very well suited for the nature of applied problems. Beginning with the development of the multiple baseline and reversal designs (Baer, Wolf, & Risley, 1968), which are the most frequently used behavioral research designs, a number of experimental designs have been made available from which a senior researcher can select one particular design that best fits his/her research project. Such designs include the multiple probe design, alternating treatments design, changing criterion design, and a number of variations of these particular designs. It is not the purpose here to describe these designs and their appropriate experimental use, as such descriptions are available from a number of other sources (e.g. Baer et al., 1968; Kazdin, 1982). However, this section does describe how certain features of the different experimental designs either facilitate or hinder the ease with which applied research can be incorporated into human service agency work routines.

Selecting an Experimental Design that Requires the Least Amount of Research Effort

In light of the premise stressed throughout this text that conducting successful applied research in human service agencies requires a considerable amount of hard work, it is advantageous for a senior researcher to reduce the amount of work required wherever possible without detracting from the quality of the research. One method of reducing the work load is to employ an experimental design that minimizes the amount of research effort required yet still allows a research question to be answered appropriately from an experimental-control point of view. Probably, the experimental design that most frequently requires the least amount of work effort in this regard is the multiple probe design (Horner & Baer, 1978).

In order to understand the advantages of the multiple probe design in terms of reducing a senior researcher's work load on a research project, it is necessary to be familiar with the more basic experimental design from which the multiple probe was derived: the multiple baseline design (Baer et al., 1968). Using a multiple baseline experimental design, several (i.e. multiple) baseline measures are simultaneously conducted across different entities such as different settings, behaviors, experimental participants or times of day. The problem-solving intervention is then conducted with one of the entities (e.g. behaviors) while the other baseline measures continue. The dependent measure is then compared between the post-intervention condition and its preceding baseline condition as well as across the other entities (e.g. behaviors) that are still in baseline. Subsequently, the intervention is applied to the next entity and then later to the next, and so on. If the dependent measure in each entity shows a change when and only when the intervention is introduced to that particular entity, then it can be experimentally concluded that the behavior change was a function of the intervention.

An example of the use of a multiple baseline experimental design in an applied research study conducted by practitioners in a human service setting is represented by an investigation by Gruber, Reeser, and Reid (1979). The Gruber et al. study evaluated a program for teaching independent walking or pedestrian skills to profoundly mentally retarded persons in an institutional setting. As indicated in Figure 1, the dependent variable of interest was the percent of the distance between the clients' living unit and a school building that the clients walked independently. Using a multiple baseline experimental design, the travel training program was first implemented with one client, then later with another, and so on across four clients. The results presented in Figure 1 indicate that the training program was successful, because the distance independently walked increased when and only when the training program was implemented (at different times) with each client.

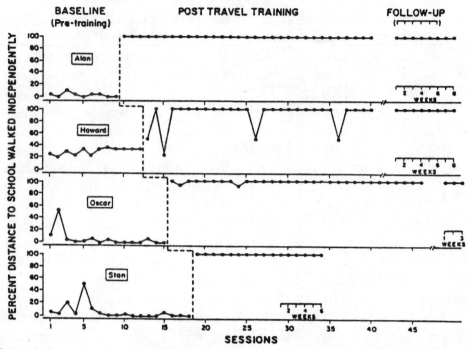

Figure 1. Example of a multiple baseline experimental design. The figure shows the percent of distance to school walked independently by each client during each observation session in baseline, following participation in a travel-training program and during follow-up. (From Gruber, B., Reeser, R., & Reid, D. H., 1979: Providing a less restrictive environment for profoundly retarded persons by teaching independent walking skills. *Journal of Applied Behavior Analysis, 12,* 285-297. Copyright by the Society for the Experimental Analysis of Behavior, Inc. Reprinted with permission.)

The multiple probe design represents a modification of the multiple baseline design that can result in a considerable time savings for an applied researcher. Basically, instead of simultaneously measuring the dependent variable across each setting (or behaviors, etc.), only intermittent probes are conducted within each setting, thereby reducing the total number of observations that must be conducted. To illustrate, Figure 2 demonstrates how, if a multiple probe design had been used in the study just noted by Gruber et al. instead of a multiple baseline design, a number of observations could have been eliminated. Each "x" in Figure 2 exemplifies where an observation could have been omitted if a multiple probe design had been used without detracting from the ability to demonstrate experimental control of the intervention. The number of observations conducted by the experimenters, and their related time and effort, could have been reduced considerably if a multiple probe design had been employed.

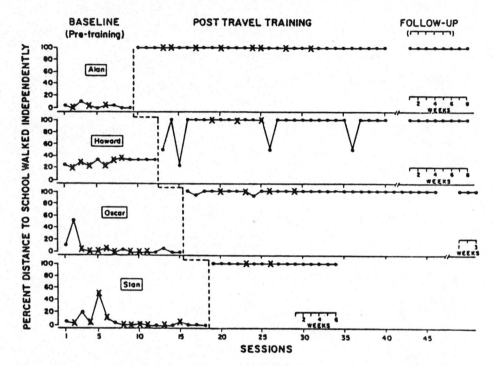

Figure 2. Example of how a multiple baseline design as previously shown in Figure 1 could be altered to represent a multiple *probe* design. Each "x" indicates where observations could have been omitted to fit the requirements of a multiple probe design—and save experimenter time and effort.

An example of how a multiple probe experimental design has actually been used in an applied research study in a human service setting is reflected in Figure 3. Figure 3 shows the results of a teacher training and supervision program that was designed to increase the amount of functional task involvement of severely handicapped students in three school classrooms (Reid et al., 1985). In this figure, the blank spaces between the data points show where observation sessions were omitted by using a multiple probe design. Each observation session that was omitted saved the researchers at least 30 minutes of time.

Because of the time and effort savings that the multiple probe design allows, use of this experimental design is strongly recommended for senior researchers wherever possible. Of course, to use either the multiple probe or multiple baseline design, the senior researcher must have several entities (e.g. settings, clients, behaviors) with which to conduct some simultaneous and near-simultaneous baseline observations and

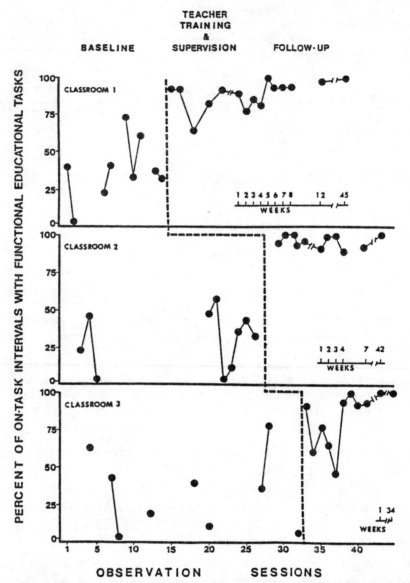

Figure 3. Example of a multiple *probe* design. The figure shows the percent of observation intervals in which severely handicapped students were engaged in functional tasks during each observation session across experimental conditions in three school classrooms. The blank spaces between data points show where observations were omitted (i.e. in contrast to if a multiple *baseline* design had been used). (From Reid, D. H., Parsons, M. B., Mc-Carn, J. E., Green, C. W., Phillips, J. F., & Schepis, M. M. (1985): Providing a more appropriate education for severely handicapped persons: Increasing and validating functional classroom tasks. *Journal of Applied Behavior Analysis, 18,* 289-301. Copyright by the Society for the Experimental Analysis of Behavior, Inc. Reprinted with permission.)

with which to subsequently and sequentially apply the problem-solving intervention. Basically, only two entities are needed to demonstrate the effectiveness of an intervention, in that once the intervention is initially accompanied by behavior change in one entity, the behavior change can subsequently be replicated with the second entity. However, in most human service settings, numerous unplanned events can occur that interfere with the opportunity to demonstrate an intervention's effectiveness with a given entity. For example, if a behavior change intervention is scheduled to be successively implemented across clients, one client may be transferred to another agency (or location within an agency) before the intervention is fully implemented with that client. Similarly, if an intervention is scheduled to be implemented across staff work units, an agency executive order may be unexpectedly directed to staff in a given work unit that conflicts with the focus of the intended intervention. Because of these types of unplanned events that can interfere with the appropriate application of a multiple probe (or multiple baseline) design, it is usually advantageous for a senior researcher to begin a study with at least three entities, and preferably four. By using three or more entities, if unplanned events interfere with the implementation of an intervention with one entity, other entities are available with which to successfully continue the research project. Identifying such entities that need improvement via an applied research intervention, be they different groups of clients or staff, different classrooms, different wards, different client problem behaviors, different times of day, etc., is usually not very difficult in most human service agencies.

In addition to the time-efficiency advantage of the multiple probe experimental design, this particular behavioral research design, like the multiple baseline from which it was derived, also frequently has the advantage of facilitating the senior researcher's task of applying the experimental intervention. That is, instead of having to intervene simultaneously with all entities that are in need of improvement within a human service agency, an applied researcher can intervene with only one entity at a time. The latter approach requires a smaller time investment by the senior researcher at any one point in time which can be advantageous when considering the numerous service responsibilities within human service agencies that continuously demand the senior researcher's attention. By intervening with only one entity at a time, it is easier for the senior researcher to muster the time and/or resources to solve the problems with that particular entity and then later, when time permits, repeat the process with the next entity.

Selecting Experimental Designs that can be Sequentially Altered with Successive Attempts to Resolve a Problem

On several occasions in this text it has been noted that an important advantage of applied behavioral research designs is that they are well suited for application within the characteristic operations of human service agencies. One of the best examples of this feature of behavioral experimental designs is that they allow an applied researcher to try successive attempts to solve a given agency problem and still be able to experimentally demonstrate which of the attempts is successful. To illustrate, sometimes the first experimental intervention a senior researcher applies to solve a given agency problem is not successful. Instead of having to abandon the research project as a failure at that point, a conscientious researcher can evaluate what went wrong with the experimental intervention and attempt another solution. If a behavioral research design is used appropriately, such a successive-intervention approach can subsequently result in a very successful applied research project. To use a behavioral design appropriately in this regard means in essence that several *controlled replications* of the effective intervention must be conducted once an effective intervention is identified during the course of the study.

Essentially, the replication of behavior change following (and only following) the application of a given problem-solving intervention represents the experimental control component of behavioral research designs such as the multiple probe and multiple baseline designs. That is, the component within behavioral experimental designs that allows for a conclusion that it was the senior researcher's intervention that was responsible for solving the problem at hand in contrast to an unplanned extraneous variable is *repeated demonstrations* of behavior change once the problem-solving intervention is applied. In those studies, for example, in which one intervention is designed and sequentially implemented across clients, or times of day, settings, and so on as exemplified earlier in Figures 1 and 3, behavior change must be replicated each time the intervention is applied in order to conclude that the intervention was responsible for the change in the given dependent variable. However, as indicated previously, sometimes an applied researcher's intervention is not effective or is only partially effective. In such cases it is then the senior researcher's task to: (a) continue trying different interventions in order to eventually resolve the targeted agency problem in one situation; and (b) once an intervention appears to be accompanied by desirable behavior change with that one situation, *replicate* the effect with other situations to experimentally demonstrate that it was indeed the intervention that was responsible for the behavior change.

An example of the process just described from an applied research project conducted by practitioners in a human service setting is reflected in Figure 4. Figure 4 presents the amount of appropriate dancing observed among mentally retarded persons across successive dance sessions during several experimental conditions (Lagomarcino et al., 1984). The purpose of the Lagomarcino et al. investigation was to evaluate a method of teaching appropriate dance skills to institutionalized mentally retarded persons in order to enhance their acceptable participation in local community dances. Following baseline observations using a multiple probe experimental design across individual clients, a dance training program was then implemented with one client (Bernie in Figure 4). Post-training observations indicated that although Bernie's appropriate dancing improved following training relative to baseline (closed data points and solid line on Figure 4), the improvement was rather minimal. Subsequently, Lagomarcino et al. designed a second intervention — dance training with follow-up supervision — and then implemented that intervention with Bernie. This time, Bernie's appropriate dancing improved significantly (see "Post-Training Plus Supervision," Figure 4). To replicate the effects of the dance-training-and-supervision intervention in order to demonstrate the experimenal control of the intervention over the dance skills of the clients, the intervention was implemented with Linda, then later with Kyle, and then, finally, with Ben (Fig. 4). Each time the intervention was applied with each client (and only at that time), the dance performance of each respective client improved, thereby demonstrating experimental control of the dance training and supervision over the clients' dance skills.

The use of the multiple probe design as exemplified in the Lagomarcino study is probably the best experimental strategy for conducting an applied research study when several different interventions have to be attempted, whether planned or unplanned, before an effective intervention is identified. However, there is also an alternative approach via a modified reversal experimental design (Baer et al., 1968; Kazdin, 1982) when successive interventions must be applied during a study. Although the reversal design at times has some serious disadvantages in regard to use within human service settings (see discussion in next section), it can be applied in a manner analogous to the use of the multiple probe design just described in some situations.

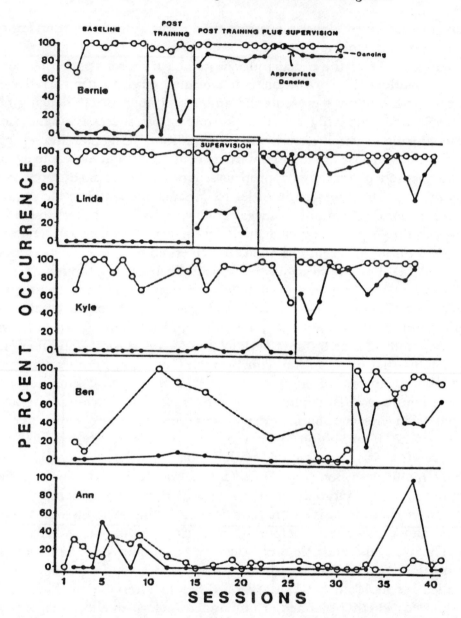

Figure 4. Example of a multiple probe design used to evalute a second intervention (post-training plus supervision) when the first intervention (post-training) was ineffective. The figure shows the percent of appropriate dancing during observations of five clients during dancing sessions across experimental conditions. (From Lagomarcino, A., Reid, D. H., Ivancic, M. T., & Faw, G. D. (1984): Leisure-dance instruction for severely and profoundly retarded persons: Teaching an intermediate community-living skill. *Journal of Applied Behavior Analysis, 17,* 71-84. Copyright by the Society for the Experimental Analysis of Behavior, Inc. Reprinted with permission.)

The reversal design is basically used by first taking baseline observations of a dependent measure with one entity, then implementing an intervention, and then reversing the conditions back to baseline by discontinuing the intervention. If the dependent measure (i.e. target behavior) changes from the initial baseline when the intervention is applied and then changes back (reverses) when the intervention is withdrawn, then it can be experimentally concluded that the intervention was responsible for the behavior change. In the case of an intervention that is *not* accompanied by behavior change and the senior researcher is conscientious about resolving the identified problem of concern, different interventions can be sequentially applied until behavior change does occur. At that point, a reversal in conditions can be conducted back to the condition (or to baseline) that preceded the intervention that was accompanied by behavior change. Consequently, the experimental control of the intervention can be established if the behavior changed during the intervention and then changed back (reversed) when the intervention was withdrawn.

An example of how a reversal experimental design can be used in the manner just described to resolve a problem when a senior researcher's first intervention is ineffective is provided by Green and Reid (1986). In this study, the experimental purpose was to identify stimuli that would function as reinforcers for multiply handicapped, profoundly mentally retarded persons who had not responded to previous habilitative programs. Different stimuli were provided contingently following a targeted behavior to see if the behavior's frequency would increase (i.e. indicate the reinforcing value of the stimulus). Figure 5 demonstrates the process with one of the participants (students) in the study. Figure 5 shows the amount of trainer assistance (prompt level) required by a student to complete a training task across training sessions, with prompt level 1 representing total assistance by the trainer and prompt level 4 representing no trainer assistance (i.e. independent completion of the task by the student). Following baseline, stimulus 1 (hug from the trainer) was evaluated for its reinforcing value during the training, with no apparent effect on the student's performance based on the prompt level required for the student to complete the task. Subsequently, a second stimulus was evaluated (stimulus 2, juice) and this stimulus *was* accompanied by improved student performance. Next, to demonstrate experimental control a reversal was conducted by withdrawing stimulus 2 and going back to the baseline condition. Once the stimulus was withdrawn, the student's performance deteriorated, indicating that it was indeed stimulus 2 that was responsible for the behavior change. The behavior change effect of stimulus 2 was then *replicated,* in that when stimulus 2 was reapplied the student's performance again improved.

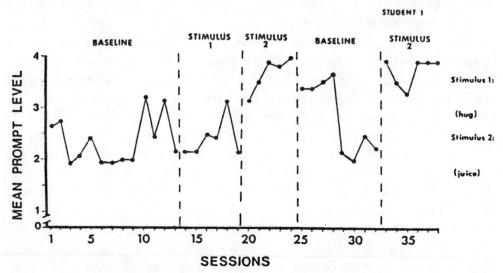

Figure 5. Example of a reversal design used to evaluate a second intervention (stimulus 2) when the first intervention (stimulus 1) was ineffective. The figure shows the mean prompt level (with 1 being the most intrusive prompt) required by a student to complete a task across training sessions for each experimental condition. (From Green, C. W., & Reid, D. H.: *Determining stimulus preference vs. reinforcer value: A comparison of strategies and outcomes.* Paper presented at the Florida Association for Behavior Analysis 6th Annual Meeting. Reprinted with permission.)

The sequence of experimental conditions as exemplified in Figure 5 essentially could have continued if stimulus 2 was found to be ineffective. Different stimuli could have been evaluated successively until one was identified that was accompanied by student behavior change. At that point, a reversal could have occurred to demonstrate experimental control of that particular intervention. However, even though this type of process is advantageous in that it allows a senior researcher to continuously try different interventions to resolve an identified agency problem and still demonstrate experimental control of a given intervention's effectiveness, for reasons discussed in the next section usually the multiple probe approach with repeated intervention attempts described earlier is a better choice than the reversal experimental design in terms of being applicable within most human service settings.

Experimental Designs to Avoid

The discussion to this point has focused on experimental research designs that are particularly advantageous for senior researchers to use in applied behavioral research in human service settings. There are also several experimental designs that frequently can be quite *disadvantageous*. The difficulties with the research designs to be discussed are not necessarily due to flaws in the designs from an experimental-control point of view but, rather, are due to practical problems in using the designs appropriately when applied in research projects in human service settings.

Avoiding Reversal Designs in Certain Situations

In the preceding description of how a reversal design could be used to fit the experimental requirements necessary to evaluate a multiple-intervention approach to resolving an agency problem, it was noted that there were some problems in using this design. In this particular case, some of the problems are inherent in the nature of the design itself. For example, sometimes a given behavior change fails to reverse when an intervention is withdrawn because the behavior has become well established in a client's repertoire due to a highly effective treatment (see Kazdin, 1982, for discussion). Additionally, there is also one potentially major problem that is due more to the nature of human service settings than to the reversal design per se. That is, in many cases staff within a human service agency will not understand and/or appreciate withdrawing a certain intervention that appears to be effective. Even though it can be explained to staff that the withdrawal of the intervention is necessary in order to carefully evaluate the effects of the intervention, many staff will feel that if the problem that the intervention is addressing is being resolved, then the intervention should not be changed or discontinued even temporarily.

For the most part, the relatively common view of staff as just described regarding the withdrawal of an effective intervention is appropriate. There are many problems in human service agencies whose severity is such that if the problematic situation appears to be improving, then nothing should be done to intentionally risk negating that improvement. Generally, these types of situations should be considered prior to beginning on applied research project that involves the use of a reversal experimental design. If there is some speculation that a given behavior change should not be reversed over the course of an investigation, then it is incumbent upon a senior researcher to determine another experimental design to use instead of a reversal.

Avoiding Changing Criterion Designs

Another behavioral research design that is probably best to avoid in applied research in human service settings is the changing criterion design. In many ways, this design is rather complex in terms of what must occur experimentally in order for the design to be used appropriately. In using a changing criterion experimental design, an applied senior researcher not only has to have an effective intervention, he/she must be able to differentially control the *degree* of effectiveness of the intervention in order to be able to change the occurrence of target behaviors at successive time intervals to predesignated criterion levels. Due to the various unplanned events that occur within human service agencies that can interfere with an intervention's effectiveness as discussed earlier, such precise control is frequently not possible. A more in-depth discussion of the intricacies of the changing criterion design is provided by Kazdin (1982). Suffice it to say here that for the changing criterion design to be applied appropriately, the senior researcher must have more control over a number of extraneous variables that can affect the exact degree of an intervention's effectiveness than what is usually possible in a human service setting. The variety of day-to-day fluctuations in the operation of most human service agencies can wreak havoc on a research project that uses an experimental design (such as the changing criterion design) that requires very close adherence to a number of precise pre-planned set of events.

A Final Technicality to Avoid

In addition to certain experimental designs that are best avoided whenever possible in applied research in human service agencies, there is another common experimental procedure that is best to avoid at all times. Specifically, whereas traditional research protocol refers to experimental participants as "subjects," this term should be avoided in research in human service settings for two primary reasons. First, due to the nature of applied, problem-solving research as discussed throughout this text, the experimental participants in a study really are not "subjects." Rather, they are what they normally are, either staff or clients. Good applied behavioral research does not require removing persons from their normal routine in order to participate as "subjects" in a research-contrived situation; good research fits the experimental procedures to the normal routine of staff and/or clients and solves whatever problem is being addressed within the typical environment in which the problem regularly occurs.

The second reason to avoid the term "subjects," as well as all the other actions between a researcher and experimental participants that the term connotes, is due to the potential impact of the term on some clients, and particularly on human service staff. In short, many people do not like being referred to as "subjects," and to refer to them in this manner is likely to cause a senior researcher to have some disgruntled individuals involved in his/her research. Sincere concern for, and awareness of, the feelings of staff and clients has to be a priority for an applied researcher (as well as any professional in a human service agency) and, in this case, simply avoiding reference to "subjects" can prevent some unnecessary disgruntlement.

REFERENCES

Baer, D. M., Wolf, M. M., & Risley, T. R. (1968). Some current dimensions of applied behavior analysis. *Journal of Applied Behavior Analysis, 1,* 91-97.

Barlow, D. H., & Herson, M. (1984). *Single case experimental designs: Strategies for studying behavior change* (2nd ed.). New York: Pergamon Press.

Burg, M. M., Reid, D. H., & Lattimore, J. (1979). Use of a self-recording and supervision program to change institutional staff behavior. *Journal of Applied Behavior Analysis, 12,* 363-375.

Dorsey, M. F., Iwata, B. A., Reid, D. H., & Davis, P. H. (1982). Protective equipment: Continuous and contingent application in the treatment of self-injurious behavior. *Journal of Applied Behavior Analysis, 15,* 217-230.

Green, C. W. & Reid, D. H. (1986). *Determining stimulus preference vs. reinforcer value: A comparison of strategies and outcomes.* Paper presented at the Florida Association for Behavior Analysis 6th Annual Meeting, Orlando FL.

Gruber, B., Reeser, R., & Reid, D. H. (1979). Providing a less restrictive environment for profoundly retarded persons by teaching independent walking skills. *Journal of Applied Behavior Analysis, 12,* 285-297.

Horner, R. D., & Baer, D. M. (1978). Multiple-probe technique: A variation of the multiple baseline design. *Journal of Applied Behavior Analysis, 11,* 189-196.

Hutchison, J. M., Jarman, P. H., & Bailey, J. S. (1980). Public posting with a habilitation team: Effects on attendance and performance. *Behavior Modification, 4,* 57-70.

Iwata, B. A., Bailey, J. S., Brown, K. M., Foshee, T. J., & Alpern, M. (1976). A performance-based lottery to improve residential care and training by institutional staff. *Journal of Applied Behavior Analysis, 9,* 417-431.

Kazdin, A. E. (1982). *Single-case research designs: Methods for clinical and applied settings.* New York: Oxford University Press.

Lagomarcino, A., Reid, D. H., Ivancic, M. T., & Faw, G. D. (1984). Leisure-dance instruction for severely and profoundly retarded persons: Teaching an intermediate community-living skill. *Journal of Applied Behavior Analysis, 17,* 71-84.

Montegar, C. A., Reid, D. H., Madsen, C. H., & Ewell, M. D. (1977). Increasing institutional staff-to-resident interactions through inservice training and supervisor approval. *Behavior Therapy, 8,* 533-540.

Reid, D. H., Parsons, M. B., McCarn, J. E., Green, C. W., Phillips, J. F., & Schepis, M. M. (1985). Providing a more appropriate education for severely handicapped persons: Increasing and validating functional classroom tasks. *Journal of Applied Behavior Analysis, 18,* 289-301.

Reid, D. H., & Whitman, T. L. (1983). Behavioral staff management in institutions: A critical review of effectiveness and acceptability. *Analysis and Intervention in Developmental Disablities, 3,* 131-149.

Shoemaker, J., & Reid, D. H. (1980). Decreasing chronic absenteeism among institutional staff: Effects of a low-cost attendance program. *Journal of Organizational Behavior Management, 2,* 317-328.

van den Pol, R. A., Reid, D. H., & Fuqua, R. W. (1983). Peer training of safety-related skills to institutional staff: Benefits for trainers and trainees. *Journal of Applied Behavior Analysis, 16,* 139-156.

Chapter 6

MAINTAINING CONSISTENT RESEARCH PRODUCTIVITY: MAKING RESEARCH FUN

IN CHAPTER 1 the importance of publishing the outcome of an applied research endeavor was stressed. In short, the ultimate test of the success of a research project is whether or not it results in a published product. However, the merits of publishing a given research project notwithstanding, an even more successful outcome of an applied researcher's efforts in a human service setting is to *consistently* publish results of research over extended periods of time; to develop and maintain a research *program* in contrast to an isolated research project.

Developing a successful research program entails conducting a series of investigations that results in a consistent outcome of published journal articles. The advantages of developing a successful research program essentially are the same as those discussed in Chapter 1 regarding the basic benefits of doing applied research in human service settings in general. However, because a program of research involves much more activity and results in more outcome than a single research project, the benefits of conducting a program of research are considerably more significant than the benefits of conducting an isolated study or two. Perhaps, the biggest advantage in this regard is that a program of research usually results in a much more thorough resolution of a human service agency's problem, as well as a more comprehensive resolution to a research question, than does a single investigation.

An example of a successful program of research in a human service setting is represented by a series of investigations conducted to improve educational services offered to severely handicapped students. A group of senior educators at Western Carolina Center (Green et al., 1986b; Green et al., 1986a; Parsons et al., 1986; Reid et al., 1985; Reid et al.,

1986) collaborated on a research program to improve the functional utility of educational services provided to severely handicapped students. (See Chapter 2 for a discussion of how the research was initiated in order to resolve an agency problem.) Initially, Green et al. (1986b) conducted a normative study involving 43 classrooms across 11 public and institutional school programs to empirically document that indeed there was a widespread problem with lack of purposeful educational tasks for severely handicapped students. Next, an investigation was conducted to demonstrate on a small scale the *effectiveness* of a staff management strategy for improving the functional utility of educational tasks provided in three classrooms serving severely handicapped persons (Reid et al., 1985). Subsequently, the *generality* of the supervisory program was then enhanced by demonstrating its effectiveness in three other classrooms serving a different type of severely handicapped student population (Green et al., 1986a). Finally, a study was conducted on a much broader scope involving four school programs to further evaluate the effectiveness, generality (and especially the *wide-scale applicability*) of the supervisory program by focusing on large numbers of staff and students over an extended period of time (Parsons et al., 1987).

Each of the four studies just summarized represented a successful applied research undertaking within a human service setting in its own right. However by continuing to address a given problem area through successive investigations, the problem area (in this case, lack of meaningful educational tasks in school programs for the severely handicapped) was more thoroughly resolved than if only one of the investigations had taken place. Also, the general *types* of topics addressed in the successive studies represent a good generic model for developing a relatively long-term program of applied research in a human service setting. Specifically, the research began by *documenting the widespread existence of a problem* and then demonstrating a method of *resolving the problem on a small scale*. Subsequently, the application of the problem-solving strategy was expanded on a *large scale* to a number of settings experiencing the same type of problem. Hence, before attempting the more comprehensive task of improving services in a large number of settings, the problem-solving strategy was developed and refined on a relatively restricted basis. Such an approach not only can result in a series of good studies, it also helps to maximize an applied researcher's time utilization by ensuring he/she has an effective intervention *prior* to taking on the difficult and very effortful task of working with numerous intervention sites. This approach of experimentally demonstrating how to solve a problem in a human service agency by addressing a small part of the agency's service provision and then applying the empirically derived strategy throughout the entire agency (or agencies) could be used as a model for long-term research programs involving a number of problem situations in human service settings.

The research program just described encompassed approximately a five-year period from the time the initial investigation began until the time the final study was published. Such an amount of time is not very unusual for the successful completion of a multi-project research undertaking. Consequently, a senior researcher must be patient and be willing to commit him/herself for a considerable period of time in order to conduct a successful program of research. Further, consistent with the basic premise that conducting applied research within a human service setting requires a significant degree of effort, a senior researcher must be consistently diligent over many months and years if he/she wants to direct a successful program of research. Fortunately, though, there are ways that a program of research can be developed and maintained within a human service agency such that the process can be reasonably managed by a senior researcher as well as be rather enjoyable. It is the purpose of this chapter to discuss how a research program can be conducted and how the undertaking can be made enjoyable.

Prior to discussing practical strategies for maintaining a program of research, the *disadvantages* of this approach to research relative to conducting independent, relatively circumscribed studies warrant mentioning. A discussion of some of the difficulties with sequential, multi-experiment programs of research was provided in Chapter 2. To briefly summarize here, because of the long time period involved, developing and maintaining this type of research program requires overcoming numerous obstacles (e.g. turnover among staff research collaborators) that can hinder successful outcomes. Consequently, it is recommended that if a senior researcher is just beginning to conduct research in a human service agency, he/she should first conduct short-term, independent investigations and achieve some success in systematically resolving a few agency problems and publishing several separate studies. Once some success has been obtained by the senior researcher and his/her colleagues, then a long-term program of research should be initiated. At that point, the senior researcher and the staff collaborators have sharpened important research skills through experience and, because of the improved skills (and probably increased interest in research among staff members due to having had some success with research), conducting a long-term research program will be easier to accomplish for all involved persons. In particular, whereas it was noted earlier (Chap. 2) that a senior researcher should conduct as much of the implementation aspects of a study him/herself as possible when first beginning research activities in a human service agency, after a project or two has been completed the senior researcher will not need to spend as much time actually conducting experimental procedures, because his/her staff will have acquired the necessary skills (and interest) to be more actively involved.

In many ways, the foundation in terms of strategies for developing a long-term program of applied research has already been discussed. Focusing research activities on the resolution of key agency problems, for example, (Chap. 2) and integrally involving competent agency staff in research efforts (Chap. 3) are essential components. However, developing a program of research also requires specific actions on the part of an applied researcher beyond what has already been discussed. These actions include how a researcher organizes his/her research activities and how components are built into the activities to increase the likelihood that they will persist over time.

Organizing Activities to Develop a Long-Term Research Program

Conducting applied research in human service settings involves three basic sets of activities: (a) planning the investigation, (b) conducting the investigation, and (c) writing up the results of the investigation. In completing a given study, each of these sets of activities occurs in the temporal sequence as just listed. In constrast, if a *program* of research is to occur, each of these activities (as they relate to separate investigations) should occur simultaneously. In essence, the best way to ensure that a consistent, long-term research program will take place, as well as to continuously improve an agency's services, is for a senior researcher to always be planning a study, be conducting another study, and be writing up a third study.

The organizational approach just described may appear at first glance to be an overwhelming task for an applied researcher, especially when considering the service responsibilities of the human service agency in which he/she works. Actually, however, if the process is organized and carried out appropriately, then the task is not unreasonable to manage. For one thing, each of the three activities does not have to be attended to by the senior researcher on a daily basis; typically only the actual implementation phase of a research program requires daily attention by the senior researcher (Chap. 2). The planning and writing components usually can be attended to on a weekly basis and still proceed at a relatively quick pace. Relatedly, there are ways to schedule time for planning and writing (Chap. 7) in order to efficiently coordinate these tasks with other research tasks and service responsibilities of an applied researcher.

Probably, the most advantageous means of simultaneously working on (at least within a week's period of time) the three sets of research activities just noted is to integrally involve other agency staff members in the process. Chapters 2 and 3 discussed a number of methods for successfully involving human service personnel in applied research activities. In regard to the three major components of a research program under discussion here, the best component for involving agency staff is the actual conducting of the experimental procedures. Typically, agency staff have more skills and experience applicable to conducting applied research procedures under the direction of the senior researcher relative to participating in the technical aspects of planning and writing up a research project. An applied researcher can have all three sets of research activities underway by focusing some of his/her attention intermittently on planning a new study across several work weeks (with input on target research questions from agency staff), overseeing the implementation of ongoing research procedures that are conducted primarily by his/her agency staff by spending a little time with the staff and/or with the resulting research data on a daily basis (Chap. 2), and spending several hours every three to four days writing up a project.

A somewhat common problem that arises when attempting to involve agency staff in the three major components of a program of research is an overemphasis on their involvement in the writing component. Writing research papers in a manner suitable for publication is one of the most difficult research skills to teach to individuals who have not had graduate-level training in research methodology, and teaching those types of skills within the ongoing operation of a human service agency is especially difficult. Chapter 7 discusses why writing is difficult as well as some suggestions for facilitating writing tasks. Because of the difficulty in this regard, a senior researcher really should not expect that his/her research colleagues will be able to assist very much with the writing component. Rather, in terms of maintaining successful research productivity over time, for the sake of efficiency a senior researcher should assume the responsibility of doing the bulk of the writing tasks necessary for preparing research papers.

The importance of a senior researcher assuming the major responsibility for completing the writing component in a program of research is particularly germane in regard to preparing the introductory and discussion sections (Chap. 7) of a research paper. In contrast, in some cases, a staff research colleague can write the essential parts of an initial draft or two of the methods and results sections. However, even in the latter cases, a senior researcher usually is required to edit the initial drafts quite extensively such that it may be more efficient for a senior researcher to write the entire paper. One exception to a senior researcher's role in doing essentially all of the writing of research papers is when he/she has worked with a given staff member on several research projects. As agency staff members become more experienced in applied research activities through participation in research projects, their ability to assist with writing tasks can increase significantly.

By using the simultaneous planning-conducting-writing approach to applied research as just described, an applied researcher can develop a consistent research program relatively quickly. Once this approach has been in place for several years, the senior researcher will probably find him/herself in a self-perpetuating research process. Specifically, across a three- to four-month period, the senior researcher will probably see a project completed in terms of the final data being collected, submit a paper for publication, receive word from a journal editor regarding the editoral decision on another paper that was previously submitted for publication and, if sound research is being conducted, read an article that he/she has just had published in a current journal issue. In addition, the senior researcher (as well as his/her collaborating agency staff) will probably receive correspondence from other professionals seeking reprints of various write-ups and/or additional information regarding a given study. Each of these events can be very rewarding and exciting for a senior researcher and his/her staff research co-workers, which in turn often stimulates the continuation of research efforts as well as the development of new research undertakings. As discussed in the next section, an applied researcher and his/her collaborating staff members *must* receive significant rewards if they are to successfully maintain a consistent research program.

Obtaining Reinforcement for Research Involvement: Making Research Fun

In any undertaking that requires a considerable amount of time and effort, an individual typically must be rewarded rather significantly for the work if he/she is going to successfully persist over time. Conducting a good applied research program in a human service setting is no exception. Fortunately, as discussed in Chapter 1, there are some very potent rewards for professionals who conduct successful applied research, with the ultimate reward of the satisfaction of having contributed a permanent part of history (e.g. a journal article) that can be used by others in the helping professions. However, the satisfaction of a published product comes a long time after a given study has been planned, conducted and written up — sometimes several years from the time the original research idea was conceived. Of course, once a research program is successfully underway for several years, the rewards associated with contributing to a professional field come considerably more frequently than when a research program is just beginning as noted in the preceding section. Nevertheless, such professional rewards will not come on a daily (or even weekly or monthly) basis, especially for new researchers. Consequently, if a successful applied research program is to be maintained over time, a senior researcher must take his/her own steps to reinforce research involvement on a much more frequent basis than what results from the formal publication process. The basic idea is to structure enough reinforcing events into the research activity on a frequent basis such that research involvement becomes *fun;* people are much more likely to stay actively involved in something if that involvement represents a good time.

Periodically, throughout this text the importance of agency staff participation in research activity with the senior researcher has been stressed. Without competent staff involvement, it is quite unlikely that a senior researcher could successfully complete a research project while working in a human service setting, and it is virtually impossible to conduct a long-term program of research. Hence, the primary goal of a senior researcher in terms of structuring reinforcing events into research activity is to make the *research involvement of agency staff very rewarding.*

Reinforcing Agency Staff for Participation in Research. There are a number of features inherent in the day-to-day activities of a good applied research project that can make the involvement of agency staff rather rewarding. This is especially the case if a senior researcher works with staff who meet the priority characteristics of effective research collaborators as described in Chapter 3. In particular, for staff who are sincerely concerned about client welfare, their recognition that client services have been improved due to the results of an applied research endeavor that they have been integrally involved in can be quite rewarding to the staff. Nevertheless, it is usually wise for a senior researcher to actively structure reinforcing events into staff's participation in research beyond what is inherently involved in research activities. There are basically two types of strategies a senior researcher can use to provide such events: formal and informal processes.

Formal Means of Reinforcing Staff Participation in Research. There are several formal means of reinforcing participation of agency staff in applied research activities. One such method is to arrange for staff to have the opportunity to travel to professional conferences and conventions in order to formally share their work with other practitioners and researchers. (Chapter 7 discusses the benefits of professional conference participation as well as pointers regarding which conferences are most advantageous.)

In using professional conferences as a source of reinforcement for staff participation in research, certain actions are required of the senior researcher to ensure that conferences fulfill this purpose. Specifically, if agency staff are to be *significantly* reinforced for presenting their research at conferences, then they must be able to present their information in a competent manner. Because most staff members are inexperienced in such activities (e.g. public speaking before a group of professional practitioners and researchers), they will usually require assistance in learning how to formally present research projects competently. It is incumbent upon the senior researcher to provide that assistance.

In regard to assisting staff research co-workers with conference presentations, the public speaking process can be viewed as a set of research-related behaviors that can be acquired by staff like most other research skills. For example, one useful strategy for helping inexperienced staff is to use the following step-wise process. First the content of the presentation is prepared in written format by the staff member(s) who will be presenting at the conference and the senior researcher, with the latter doing the bulk of the writing. Second, the staff member who will be delivering the presentation at the conference practices presenting the main components of the paper by him/herself. Third, once the staff member feels relatively comfortable about knowing what he/she is going to say, the staff member then practices the presentation in front of the senior researcher. Fourth, the senior researcher provides feedback to the staff person and the process is repeated until both the staff person and the senior researcher believe the presentation is well organized and well articulated. Next, the staff member practices the presentation in the exact format that it will be delivered at the conference in front of a small group of other agency staff members (including the senior researcher) who are asked to provide constructive feedback to the presenting staff person.

In conjunction with the first five steps of preparing a staff member's conference involvement, visual aides (primarily photographic slides) can be incorporated into the presentation process. For example, slides of research participants, the research settings, graphs of the results, and so on, can be made and incorporated into the presentation practice routine. Well-prepared slides not only enhance the impact of the presentation by making it easier to understand and more interesting, slides can also make the presenter's task easier by helping to cue him/her as to what material to discuss at various points in the presentation. In addition, sometimes the use of slides can help reduce the presenter's initial anxiety during a speech by drawing the audience's attention away from the presenter momentarily and toward the slides.

One drawback of the presentation preparation process just described is that it is relatively time consuming for the staff person and the senior researcher. However, the time and effort are usually worthwhile, because the process can be quite useful in helping the staff member present the most appropriate content of the research project and to do so with an effective speaking style. The practice routine, especially the practice in front of other staff persons, can also help to lessen the anxieties that often accompany initial public speaking endeavors as well as give the staff person needed confidence. Such features are important, because, again, if an agency staff person is to be reinforced by others via presenting his/her research at a professional conference, then the presentation must be well done; a research project that is poorly presented will usually result in more unpleasant consequences for a staff person than rewards.

If an applied research project is indeed well presented by a staff member at a professional conference, the experience is almost always very rewarding for the staff person. Typically, feedback from the audience will clearly demonstrate to the staff person that his/her research efforts are well appreciated. However, as a point of caution, a senior researcher should be careful to ensure that the rewarding experience of the conference presentation does not overshadow or interfere with the final major step in conducting successful research: publishing the study. A frequent set of events in this regard that occurs rather inadvertently is that: (a) considerable effort goes into preparing and giving a conference presentation, (b) the staff member (and senior researcher) is heavily rewarded at the conference, and (c) there is a long period of time before any effort is subsequently put into writing up the research for submission for publication consideration by a journal.

The time lag that frequently occurs between a conference presentation and the submission of a paper for publication is due to several factors. As just alluded to, the conference presentation functions as a rewarding experience which, in essence, can have the impact of leading the presenting staff member and the senior researcher to believe that they have achieved their goal with the research and, hence, have completed the work on the project. In addition, because of the relatively effortful process of preparing for the presentation, the researchers are ready for a break in their work load following the conference. Nevertheless, a senior researcher needs to keep in mind that the rewarding experience of the conference presentaton is relatively short-lived. Conference presentations usually do not result in permanent contributions to a professional discipline as do journal articles. Relatedly, the perception created by the rewarding presentation experience at the conference that a research project is completed is false; a research project is not successfully completed until it is published.

The best strategy for preventing the delay in completing the writing process that is necessary to submit a paper for publication is to submit the paper *prior* to the conference presentation. A senior researcher should establish a general operating rule with his/her staff research collaborators that conference presentations (and the opportunity to travel to the conference site) will not be allowed unless the paper describing the research project to be presented at the conference has been submitted for publication. Such a process not only prevents unnecessary delays in completing a paper that often follow conference presentations, the process also can enhance the presentation by causing the material that is to be presented to be better organized (i.e. by having the material in final form via the completed paper).

In addition to conference presentations, a rather formal means of reinforcing agency staff for their participation in applied research is through official awards provided within a given agency. For example, Western Carolina Center uses the "Director's Award For Outstanding Research" as a means of formally recognizing research efforts. Periodically, staff at Western Carolina Center who participated in a research endeavor are recognized for their contribution and awarded a formal certificate (see example in Figure 6). Relatedly, an annual awards banquet is held at the center in which agency staff are also recognized for their participation in research activities.

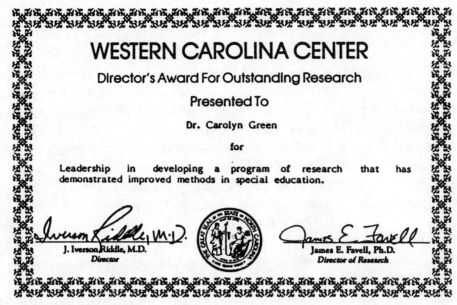

WESTERN CAROLINA CENTER

Director's Award For Outstanding Research

Presented To

Dr. Carolyn Green

for

Leadership in developing a program of research that has demonstrated improved methods in special education.

J. Iverson Riddle, M.D.
Director

James E. Favell, Ph.D.
Director of Research

Figure 6. Example of a formal means of recognizing research involvement within an agency. The award was developed by Iverson Riddle and Jim Favell of Western Carolina Center.

Perhaps the most readily available means of formally recognizing staff for their participation in applied research is for the senior researcher to prepare an agency memorandum that expresses appreciation to a staff person for his/her competent involvement in a research project. The memorandum can be copied to appropriate senior-level staff as well as the staff member's official personnel file and be subsequently used as documentation of the valuable service that the employee has performed for the agency and its clients. Of course, as with essentially any type of interpersonal expression of appreciation, the senior researcher must be sincere in his/her recognition statements to a collaborating staff member if the statements are to be well received by the staff person.

In using agency-specific means of formally recognizing staff participation in research like those just described, a certain degree of caution should be taken similar to that with conference presentations in regard to overemphasizing the importance of the recognition. This is particularly the case with formal awards (e.g. Fig. 6). At times, individuals within an agency become a little too preoccupied with their own local recognition systems and lose sight of the main reason for conducting research: to improve the helping professions by disseminating useful information, as well as to enhance a given agency's service provision. Hence, senior researchers and collaborating staff should not become overly concerned about local awards to the extent that the importance of publishing the results of research endeavors is diminished. Awards should be used to provide extra enjoyment while an applied researcher and his/her staff are en route to maintaining a successful applied research program that results in consistent publication of research results. Agency awards should not be used as a final goal attainment.

Informal Means of Reinforcing Staff Participation in Research. In addition to formal awards and recognition processes as a means of reinforcing staff participation in research (and, subsequently, making research involvement more enjoyable for staff), there are a number of rather informal means. One such means that is usually inherent in good applied research, as alluded to earlier, is that if the research targets an agency problem that the staff member(s) recognizes as a truly important problem, then involvement in research is likely to be rewarding for staff. Staff will appreciate the efforts that go into resolving the problem through the research project and will achieve satisfaction in seeing the problem actually resolved. In this regard, as discussed earlier in Chapter 2, a research topic is most likely to address a relevant agency problem from the point of view of agency staff if those staff are integrally involved in initially determining the purpose of the research.

One rather interesting means of making staff participation in research enjoyable is to periodically make the research activities somewhat different from what occurs on a routine workday basis within the human service agency. For example, one approach that the author learned from Jon Bailey at Florida State University is to hold social/research meetings. Approximately once per month an evening research meeting is held at a staff member's house. A group of staff who are involved in research within an agency bring their own refreshments and meet to discuss: (a) an idea for a research project, (b) the current results and procedural issues of an ongoing project, and/or (c) the results and conclusions of a completed project. By meeting during non-work time away from the work site in a cordial atmosphere, often the meeting and idea-sharing process can be more relaxed and enjoyable than a routine meeting during the workday. However, to ensure that the meeting serves a functional research purpose and does not turn into solely a social gathering, usually the senior researcher must assume the responsibility of structuring the meeting, preparing a simple agenda in terms of which staff person(s) will present their research material at the meeting, and disseminating information to the appropriate persons regarding when and where the meeting will occur and what the agenda will be.

If informal research meetings as just described develop into an (enjoyable) process that becomes a regular event, then the meetings can provide an excellent learning opportunity for staff. In particular, one of the most educational aspects is for staff research collaborators to be able to observe, across a number of meetings, the conception of a research idea by a staff person, the development of the experimental procedures and the accompanying results of the project, and, eventually, read the final product in manuscript form or as a journal article. Such an experience is an excellent means of demonstrating to new research staff what the complete process of doing applied research involves, as well as showing other staff who are working diligently on a current project that indeed there is an eventual outcome to all of their efforts.

A less direct means of attempting to make staff involvement in research enjoyable is to provide extra personnel assistance to staff who are conscientiously conducting research. That is, it can be very helpful (and, consequently, reinforcing) to some staff for the senior researcher to recognize that they are working very diligently and to find a way to provide extra person power to assist with the research work and thereby lessen the work load of the collaborating staff members. Methods of finding extra personnel assistance are discussed in Chapter 4. For many staff persons, the extra help will be appreciated not only because it lessens their work load in completing the research endeavor but also because if the research is appropriately focused as described earlier, the extra assistance is helpful in fulfilling important service responsibilities of the staff persons.

Reinforcing a Senior Researcher for Research Activity

In many ways, more attention should be directed to methods of making agency staff participation in research enjoyable than to methods of making the senior researcher's participation reinforcing. Directing primary attention to staff involvement in this regard is warranted when considering that the senior researcher usually has more initial motivation to conduct research because of his/her more extensive training background and/or experience in conducting applied research. However, the senior researcher should not neglect his/her own enjoyment factor — a factor that sometimes is relatively forgotten during the months of patient and diligent work that are required to successfully complete an applied research project in a human service agency. Fortunately, however, there are several potentially potent sources of reinforcement for a senior researcher inherent in conducting successful applied research, especially if some of the basic principles presented in this text are adhered to. As with staff enjoyment with research involvement, perhaps the most powerful reinforcer, if the basic premise of placing the agency's service mission as top priority is kept in mind, is witnessing an important agency problem resolved through an applied research endeavor with subsequent improvement in client services. In this respect, the emphasis on observable and objective data that is an integral part of applied behavioral research frequently has the effect of making improvements in client services that result from a research project much more visible within a human service agency than what typically occurs in terms of routine (non-research) attempts to improve service provision.

Another source of enjoyment from research activities for a senior researcher is the close work involvement with competent and energetic staff persons. As discussed in Chapter 3, an applied researcher should strive to collaborate on research projects with the most competent staff members within a given human service agency. Further, where possible, the senior researcher should involve staff persons who are skilled interpersonally. Working with proficient and pleasant research partners not only enhances the likelihood of a successful research project but also makes the day-to-day research work routine more enjoyable for the senior researcher. (See chapter 3 regarding priority characteristics of effective research collaborators.)

Working with competent and interpersonally skillful staff persons on research projects also has a rather indirect benefit for the senior researcher. In many human service settings, a senior researcher has numerous demands on his/her time, especially if the senior researcher is in an upper-level authoritative position within the agency's organizational hierarchy. Invariably, those demands do not draw a senior researcher's attention to research activity; rather, the demands draw attention (and usually rightfully so if the senior researcher is attending to the agency's service responsibilities) to more routine, non-research problems on such diverse topics as, for example, staff absenteeism, bureaucratic sluggishness in hiring and promoting staff, shortfalls in specific budget items, emergency interventions with clients in a crisis situation, and unexpected directives from superiors. One means of helping to ensure that the senior researcher does not become *totally* engulfed with such demands is to work with highly proficient staff persons as research collaborators. Such staff usually have an effective manner of attracting the researcher's attention, albeit if even for only a few minutes per day, to help the staff with a particular problem they are having with an ongoing research project. In short, competent staff will usually take it upon themselves to (pleasantly) insist that the senior researcher attend to their project because they are not likely to let a research project (or any significant agency work responsibility with which they are involved) become sloppy or ineffective due to a lack of direction. In such cases a senior researcher will usually find him/herself being grateful in the long run to a collaborating staff person for directing the former's attention to an ongoing research project, which represents something the senior researcher would like to attend to but sometimes lacks the self-control to do so because of numerous competing (non-research) demands.

The involvement of competent staff in research activities also results in another, rather subtle type of reward for a senior researcher that is specifically related to conducting a *program* of research. Staff persons who perform their agency responsibility proficiently are usually the types of individuals who learn new skills relatively quickly. As alluded to earlier, by participating in several studies as part of a program of research, these staff research collaborators will most likely develop a number of research skills such that the senior researcher can rely more heavily on the staff persons for conducting various parts of investigations. Consequently, a reward exists for the senior researcher, in that the effort required of him/her to conduct successive projects is reduced and it becomes *easier* to engage in reserch.

Another source of intermittent reinforcement that can help make a senior researcher's involvement in research enjoyable is the close contact with the data that results from an ongoing project. Of course, as discussed previously (chap. 2) it is crucial that a senior researcher stay in close contact with data stemming from a research project in order to ensure that experimental procedures are being conducted appropriately. However, because the data can be a direct representation of the improvement in an agency's service provision, the data can also be reinforcing for the senior researcher by making it apparent on a day-to-day basis that his/her efforts are succeeding in terms of making improvements within the agency. The satisfaction that stems from viewing objective data in this manner is one reason why researchers display graphs of the results of ongoing projects visibly in their offices or work stations. Such displays represent a convenient and pleasant reminder that important actions are (successfully) taking place to improve service provision (as well as indicate that competent research is underway).

As mentioned earlier in this chapter, one of the most apparent and generally powerful sources of satisfaction for a senior researcher's participation in research is the notification of acceptance of his/her work for publication. It is at this point that realization occurs that the ultimate goal in conducting applied research has been achieved: information based on the research will be made permanently available for assisting others in the helping professions. However, because not every research project ends up as it was intended, not every manuscript submitted by an applied researcher will be accepted for publication. Consequently, a senior researcher needs to be aware that the editorial decision regarding his/her applied research manuscript represents not only a potentially potent source of satisfaction, it also represents a potential source of very discouraging information. Receiving news that editorial staff do not believe that a given manuscript is worthy of publication can be quite disappointing for a senior researcher, and particularly for a new researcher.

Of course, receiving an editorial rejection from a respective journal does not prohibit submitting the manuscript to another journal for publication consideration. In actuality, it would be unwise not to submit the paper to a second journal and, if need be, to a third journal in order to ensure that a given research project receives thorough and appropriate consideration to be published. In some cases, though, a decision must be finally accepted by a senior researcher that his/her paper will not be published. If three independent journal review processes unanimously conclude that a paper should not be published, then usually a researcher should accept the fate of his/her research project at that point.

In some situations, receiving an editorial rejection as just described has actually had a rather devastating impact on senior researchers in human service settings. The disappointing news has essentially convinced applied researchers to discontinue research activities. Such an effect is somewhat understandable when considering the tremendous amount of time and effort required of an applied researcher (and collaborating staff) to progress to the point of submitting a research manuscript to a journal and then finding out that the paper will not be published. Nevertheless, some editorial decisions against acceptance of a manuscript must be expected and, therefore, a senior researcher should guard against letting an editorial rejection have too serious an impact on him/her.

One rather effective way to guard against the overly negative impact of an editorial rejection decision is to focus on the organizational strategy discussed earlier for developing a program of research in contrast to an isolated research project. To recapitulate, a senior researcher should engage in three simultaneous sets of research activities: planning a study, conducting a study, and writing up a study. If these activities are occurring, then a senior researcher can usually cope relatively easily with an editorial rejection regarding a study previously conducted. For example, because of the ongoing work when a senior researcher receives the editorial decision, he/she can focus attention on the current research endeavor in contrast to dwelling on the decision regarding past research work. Relatedly, because research activity is ongoing (e.g. writing a manuscript), the senior researcher knows he/she will soon have another opportunity to receive a favorable editorial decision when the new paper is submitted to a journal. In contrast, if research work is not ongoing and the senior researcher knows that it could easily be another year or two before another opportunity would arise in terms of designing a new study from the beginning and eventually submitting it for publication consideration, the disappointing news from the editor coupled with the thought of another year or two of work can effectively dissuade the senior researcher from attempting additional studies.

A second advantage of engaging in the three simultaneous sets of research activity in regard to coping with an editorial rejection is that the process actually allows the senior researcher to benefit from the editorial decision. Specifically, often (at least with the more reputable applied research journals) an editorial rejection letter contains specific information pertaining to how the area of research that was addressed in the rejected manuscript can be improved. Such information can be immediately relevant for a senior researcher if he/she has ongoing research activities within which the new information can be incorporated in order to improve the research and, subsequently, the publication possibilities of future manuscript submissions.

REFERENCES

Green, C. W., Canipe, V. S., Way, P. J., & Reid, D. H. (1986a). Improving the functional utility and effectiveness of classroom services for students with profound multiple handicaps. *The Journal of the Association for Persons with Severe Handicaps, 11,* 162-170.

Green, C. W., Reid, D. H., McCarn, J. E., Schepis, M. M., Phillips, J. F., & Parsons, M. B. (1986b). Naturalistic observations of classrooms serving severely handicapped persons: Establishing evaluative norms. *Applied Research in Mental Retardation, 7,* 37-50.

Parsons, M. B., Schepis, M. M., Reid, D. H., McCarn, J. E., & Green, C. W. (1987). *Expanding the impact of behavioral staff management: A wide-scale, long-term application in schools serving severely handicapped students. Journal of Applied Behavior Analysis,* in press.

Reid, D. H., Green, C. W., McCarn, J. E., Parsons, M. B., & Schepis, M. M. (1986). *Purposeful training with severely handicapped persons: A Trainer's Guidebook.* Morganton, NC, Western Carolina Center.

Reid, D. H., Parsons, M. B., McCarn, J. E., Green, C. W., Phillips, J. F., & Schepis, M. M. (1985). Providing a more appropriate education for severely handicapped persons: Increasing and validating functional classroom tasks. *Journal of Applied Behavior Analysis, 18,* 289-301.

Chapter 7

DISSEMINATING AND PUBLISHING APPLIED RESEARCH AS A HUMAN SERVICE PRACTITIONER

IN THE INTRODUCTORY comments to this book as well as in subsequent sections, it has been stressed that in order for applied research conducted in human service settings to be successful, the results of the research must be published. Unfortunately, publishing research, and gaining the valuable information that usually comes from the editorial review system that is part of the publishing process, is one of the more difficult components of conducting research in applied settings. The difficulty is due to several factors. In particular, many senior researchers do not have very much experience and/or skill in performing this aspect of research activity. Part of the problem in this regard is that most professionals who work in human service settings have not been trained very competently in how to write research papers for submission to refereed journals. Relatedly, although some senior researchers may have experience in working on research projects that previously resulted in a published article, the vast majority have no experience in *independently* completing the multi-step process involved in designing, conducting, writing and eventually publishing an applied research project. Rather, in cases where senior researchers have previously co-authored research papers, they usually have received considerable guidance and assistance from more experienced researchers such as the university faculty member(s) who directed the senior researchers' thesis or dissertation.

Another reason for the difficulty in publishing papers while working within a human service agency is that it is more difficult to synthesize manuscript writing into the routine job duties of the agency relative to other components of conducting a research project. Nevertheless, there are ways of facilitating the writing, publication and dissemination process. It is the purpose of this chapter to discuss how to go about this aspect of applied research. However, before discussing methods of facilitating the writing and publishing of research papers per se, some necessary prerequisite activities warrant discussion.

A Prerequisite for Publishing: Staying Current with Advances in the Professional Field

In Chapter 2, the importance of a practitioner staying abreast of research developments in a respective professional discipline was emphasized in regard to selecting relevant research topics. Maintaining a knowledge base about advances in a professional field is equally important when attempting to write and subsequently publish an applied research paper. In this regard, a disadvantage of working in an applied setting is that staying abreast of professional developments is not something that happens automatically in the routine course of the job, nor does it happen very easily. Whereas in college and university settings, for example, a faculty member can stay at least somewhat abreast of the field through preparations for teaching courses and interactions with colleagues who are active and knowledgeable in the professional field, such opportunities are not typically available to an applied researcher in a human service setting. Also, access to literature sources is usually more available in academic research environments than in human service agencies. Consequently, specific actions must be taken on a regular basis by a senior researcher to ensure he/she stays knowledgeable about developments in a given professional discipline.

In considering specific steps a senior researcher can take to help maintain a current knowledge base of a professional discipline, a general strategy for increasing the likelihood of success in this endeavor warrants mentioning. That is, whatever steps an applied researcher takes to expand his/her amount of relevant information, the steps should be *goal-directed* in contrast to a rather free-lance search for information. To illustrate, professionals in human service settings invariably discuss the importance of reading relevant journals or other literature sources in order to stay knowledgeable about a professional field. Almost equally frequently are complaints from the same individuals that they are dissatisfied with the infrequency with which they actually complete such reading. A major reason often provided for the difficulty in reading on a regular basis is the lack of sufficient time. Time constraints can indeed be a problem. However, a more significant reason for the difficulty is that the time spent reading is not used in a goal-directed fashion in terms of trying to fulfill a specific need from the reading and, hence, there is no discernible goal that is ever achieved. Professionals usually try to read relevant literature because it is generally assumed to be professionally advantageous to do so. Because there is no readily apparent goal that is achieved with such reading, the process becomes essentially never-ending and most senior researchers eventually discontinue their reading efforts. A more effective motivator in the long run to encourage reading of professional literature is reading in search of a specific type of information that a senior researcher is currently very interested in. For example, a good reason to review certain journal articles is to obtain background information for designing or writing up a study that a senior researcher is currently focusing on. A similar reason to engage in goal-directed reading exists if there is a unique or especially problematic staff or client issue to resolve and a senior researcher desires new ideas on how to approach the problem. As discussed later in this chapter, there are ways to seek this type of specific information from various literature sources that meets a current need of a senior researcher while at the same time increasing awareness of other developments in a professional field in general. In the following discussion of action steps regarding how to stay current on professional developments, the reader is encouraged to consider the recommendations in regard to primarily seeking specific information that he/she is currently interested in — and secondarily for enhancing a more general knowledge base about a professional discipline.

Steps for Maintaining an Up-To-Date Knowledge Base of a Professional Field: Using Professional Conferences

One of the most enjoyable means of enhancing a knowledge base regarding research and/or clinical developments in a given discipline is by attending professional conferences and conventions. Conferences provide an opportunity to see and/or hear many up-to-date research developments across a brief two- or three-day time period. Conferences also afford the opportunity to interact personally with other applied researchers to acquire in-depth information about ongoing research programs. Perhaps most advantageously, as discussed in Chapter 6, once a senior researcher and his/her staff colleagues have a research program underway in a human service agency, conferences provide a chance to present the research results to interested persons around the country and to receive rewarding and constructive feedback. Of course, for many individuals conferences are also a pleasurable experience on a more social level because of traveling to interesting places, interacting with former colleagues, and so on.

Although conferences can be enjoyable and productive professionally, there are also some problems that must be overcome in order to use conferences as a means of improving awareness of professional developments. For one thing, not all conferences have very much new information to provide due to a small number of speakers participating and/or the involvement of speakers who do not have very much useful or interesting information to provide. Experience in attending different conferences as well as questioning other practitioner-researchers who attend conferences can help determine which conferences are worth attending. From the perspective of learning about recent research happenings in applied behavior analysis, the annual convention of the Association for Behavior Analysis is quite useful. The annual convention of the Association for the Advancement of Behavior Therapy is also often useful, albeit more from a clinical point of view than an applied research perspective.

The two conferences just noted represent relatively general professional gatherings in terms of focusing on entire fields (i.e. applied behavior analysis and behavior therapy). There are also a number of conferences that have a more restricted focus that can be particularly useful for persons working in specialized types of human service settings. For example, for a professional staff person in a human service agency that serves seriously developmentally disabled individuals, specialized conferences that can be useful are the annual conference of the Association for Persons with Severe Handicaps and the annual Gatlinburg Conference on Research in Mental Retardation.

A second problem with conferences that can occur regarding their utility for upgrading professional knowledge is that often they are quite expensive (e.g. travel, lodging, registration fees). Sometimes, the expense can be reimbursed by the senior researcher's agency. Probably more frequently, though, an agency cannot (or will not) pay for all (or perhaps any) of the conference expense. Actually, in planning conference participation it is probably best to assume that an agency will not be able to reimburse expenses. Lack of funding in this regard really should not detract very seriously from a senior researcher's conference participation. The expense incurred by the researcher should be viewed as an investment in his/her professional career (some of the expense is also tax deductible). Further, a close analysis of the learning and enjoyment benefits of an individual's participation in professional conferences would probably reveal that the individual receives more benefits than his/her agency and, consequently, it seems appropriate that the individual share, or assume entirely, the cost involved.

A final problem with conference participation pertains to the impact on the human service agency of a senior researcher's absence from the agency work site while attending the conference. Because the first priority of an applied researcher within a human service agency is the service mission of the agency, the researcher must determine for each potential conference whether or not the current job demands will allow him/her to be away from work during that particular time period. Relatedly, too frequent absences from an agency for conference participation can have a bad personal-relations impact on agency staff, particularly if the agency is footing part of the expense and/or the senior researcher is on the agency's payroll while attending the conference. In many applied settings there are certain professionals with whom agency staff are frequently displeased because of their frequent absences from the facility. Sometimes, the criticism is justified, in that given professionals expend a considerable amount of an agency's travel resources without the agency receiving any significant benefit from the conference participation. However, persons who are willing to be excessively absent from an agency for conference participation or similar activities usually are the types of staff persons who do not add very much to the agency even when they are there; their primary mission is more often their own professional/personal advancement or enjoyment in contrast to the agency's service provision. In other cases, criticism that might arise regarding absence from work is not justified, in that given professionals really are not absent all that much (e.g. two or three conferences a year). In the latter cases, the displeasure that may be expressed by staff is typically short-lived and does not represent a significant problem in terms of a senior researcher using a conference to help improve his/her knowledge base in a professional field.

Steps for Maintaining an Up-To-Date Knowledge Base of a Professional Field: Selective Use of Books

Probably the most traditionally recognized method of improving a professional knowledge base is the conscientious use of professional texts. Indeed, people are often impressed with the professional library some staff members maintain in their agency offices — often viewed as a sign of staff interest in professional and scholarly developments. However, as with conferences there are also some serious problems with a heavy reliance on books as a method of maintaining a current awareness of professional developments. For example, books can be quite expensive. Also, there is a plethora of texts being published each year on topics relating to human services. Although certainly many of these books are quite helpful for an applied researcher, there are many, many others that really are not very helpful. Unfortunately, it is usually difficult to judge a text's worth until the book has been read, which, of course, can be time consuming and, in most human service agencies, means the book must first be purchased by the interested staff person or his/her agency. Related to the latter point, access to books is often a problem in many human service agencies unless a university library is close by.

A final problem with reliance on books for staying abreast of professional developments is that the information in books that pertains to specific research developments is frequently somewhat outdated by the time the book is published and made available. To illustrate, in preparing a text on behavior-modification research and application with severely and profoundly mentally retarded persons (Whitman, Scibak & Reid, 1983), two to three years were required to review, summarize and draw conclusions from the relevant literature, and approximately another year was required during the actual editorial and publication process. Consequently, by the time the text information became available in bookstores and libraries, the research that had occurred for some two years immediately prior to the book's availability was not represented in the text.

Because of the problem areas just noted, using books to help stay current on professional developments requires a careful selection process in order to avoid wasting time, effort and money. Generally, the most useful books for senior researchers in human service settings in regard to providing helpful and relatively up-to-date research information are those whose chapters focus primarily on critical reviews of existing applied research. Unfortunately, these types of texts are relatively rare among the multitude of books on the market, probably because thorough literature reviews and analyses are effortful to prepare. Nevertheless, texts that provide reviews of the research do appear periodically and it is quite useful to screen through various advertisement fliers from publishers, advertisements in journals and book displays at conferences to find these types of books. In some specialty areas in the human services there are also serial publications that provide research reviews on different topics sequentially across successive volumes. A serial publication that can be particularly helpful, for example, in the specialty areas of mental retardation and developmental disabilities is the *Advances in Developmental Disorders* (Vol. 1-3 to date) series that Rowland Barrett and Johnny Matson edit (JAI Press, publishers). The *International Review of Research in Mental Retardation* series edited by Norman Ellis (Academic Press, publisher) can be similarly helpful. On a more general level, the *Journal of Applied Behavior Analysis* (JABA) publishes a reprint volume series that presents key behavior analysis studies in selected topic areas (e.g. behavior analysis in developmental disabilities; behavior analysis in community applications) that can be very useful for providing quick access to relevant research literature.

Steps for Maintaining an Up-To-Date Knowledge Base of a Professional Field: Using Professional Journals

All things considered, probably the best way to stay abreast of research developments within a professional discipline is to read journals that publish applied research articles. Journals provide a more up-to-date source of research developments than books and also provide original research reports in contrast to someone else's summary or critique of various studies. However, a free-lance approach to staying familiar with journal articles is not recommended; rather, as discussed earlier, a goal-directed approach in terms of searching for information *specific* to a senior researcher's current area of interest and research is recommended if journal reading is to occur consistently.

As with the use of books as information sources, effective journal reading requires a careful selection process to avoid wasting time, effort and money on irrelevant information. There is a considerable number of applied research journals currently being published from which to choose, although the selection pool is more manageable with journals than with books. Given the focus of this text on applied behavior analysis, there are several journals that are particularly relevant as a source of applied behavioral research. Table 2 lists examples of such journals. In addition to the journals listed in Table 2 that publish exclusively or primarily applied behavioral research across a variety of content areas, there are many journals that publish applied behavioral research in specialty areas such as education, developmental disabilities, medical applications, environmental/ecological issues, residential service provision and industrial/organizational applications, to name a few. Appendix B provides samples of the relevant journals in these and other specialized content areas.

Table 2

Examples of Journal Sources for General Applied Behavioral Research

Journal	Publisher
Journal of Applied Behavior Analysis	Society for the Experimental Analysis of Behavior
Behavior Modification	Sage Publications
Behavior Therapy	Academic Press
Journal of Behavior Therapy and Experimental Psychiatry	Pergamon Press
Child and Family Behavior Therapy	Haworth Press
Behavior Research and Therapy	Pergamon Press

Because of the relatively large number of journals currently available that publish applied behavioral research, it is not very likely that an applied researcher in a human service setting can stay immediately abreast of every article that is published in each journal issue. A useful strategy to help in this area is the following step-wise process. First, when a new issue of a journal relevant to a current area of interest of a senior researcher is received by his/her agency, the table of contents of the journal should be quickly screened. Second, if an article appears immediately relevant for ongoing research, the paper should be highlighted and read as time permits. Third, if an article is located in the table of contents that is not necessarily related to an ongoing project but appears relevant to an area that is likely to be of interest in the future, the article should be earmarked for a secretary to photocopy and file. In this regard, one small but nevertheless important advantage of a researcher working in a human service setting, particularly in an authoritative position (Chap. 3), is better secretarial support than what is typically found in many university settings. Although there are certainly exceptions, usually a senior staff person in a human service agency has more secretarial services than a university faculty member who is more likely to be sharing secretarial services with a number of the staff. It can be very advantageous for a senior researcher to learn how to work with secre-

tarial staff to obtain their timely support in completing research-related activities such as developing and maintaining a system for quickly accessing
relevant journal articles.

One of the developments in the last decade or so that is often assumed
to be helpful in attempting to stay current on research published in professional journals is the availability of computerized literature searches.
However, the outcome of the computerized searches is not always particularly useful. These types of searches frequently result in massive listings of
articles that are not specifically relevant in regard to the information that
an applied researcher desires to obtain. Such a problem may be due to a
given researcher's inability to proficiently utilize the computerized
searches. The problem may also be due, at least in part, to imprecise and/
or inconsistent methods by which articles are originally categorized by
authors or editors within a computer bank such that, subsequently, the
manner in which the articles are grouped by content area within the computer search is not very clear. Regardless, a more useful procedure in
most situations for locating journal articles that are relevant to a senior researcher's area of interest is to use the cumulative index that many
journals now provide. For example, JABA publishes a cumulative index
in the fourth issue of each volume covering all articles in that volume. Periodically, a more comprehensive index is published such as JABA's 1977
cumulative index that covers all volumes since the journal's inception in
1968. Using such an index, articles can be quickly located on specific topics of interest and those articles in turn will lead to other relevant research
articles based on the studies that they reference.

Steps for Maintaining an Up-To-Date Knowledge Base of a Professional Field: Old-Fashioned Literature Reviews

Each of the strategies identified so far in this chapter can be helpful to
varying degrees in keeping a senior researcher abreast of research developments in a given field. However, there is one additional strategy that
is superior to all others (at least from the author's perspective). Unfortunately, the process is rather old-fashioned as well as time-consuming and
effortful. Nonetheless, as with the basic premise that doing applied research in human service settings requires hard work, doing a thorough
job of staying knowledgeable about a professional field requires considerable diligence. The strategy referred to here involves several steps.
First, several topics of serious interest on the part of the applied researcher are identified. Second, the most relevant journals related to the

identified topics are selected and made available, usually requiring a trip to a university library on the part of the senior researcher. Third, the title and/or abstract of *every article in each journal issue* covering the preceding 10-15 years is briefly scanned. Finally, those articles that relate to the topics of current (and future) interest are earmarked for subsequent photocopying, critiquing and/or filing for later reference.

To assist in ensuring the thoroughness of the literature review process just described in terms of screening *all* relevant articles, as well as enhancing the organizational efficiency of the review, a *journal review form* as exemplified in Figure 7 can be quite useful. This type of form provides a permanent record of the literature sources that have been screened such that when future occasions arise to look for relevant literature, the senior researcher has an accurate account of what he/she has already reviewed, thereby preventing needless redundancy in terms of reviewing the same journals a second time. Avoiding such duplication of effort is, of course, important from a time efficiency standpoint. Maintaining an organized record of the literature that has been searched warrants particular attention for researchers working in human service settings, because rarely can an applied researcher schedule enough time to conduct this type of literature review all at once (e.g. across several consecutive days). Rather, time for reviewing journals is usually dispersed across weeks or months in conjunction with other job responsibilities within the human service agency. When the process is spread over lengthy time periods, it is more likely that a senior researcher will forget which journals have been previously reviewed unless the form in Figure 7 or something similar is used.

Although the journal review process just described is undoubtedly time-consuming, there are some major advantages involved that seem to make the time and effort investments worthwhile. Perhaps most importantly, this approach probably represents the most thorough method of reviewing relevant literature and leaves little chance that important articles will be overlooked. In addition, even though the journals are screened for articles on specific topic areas of interest (i.e. goal-directed reviewing as described earlier), the process brings a senior researcher into contact with essentially all relevant research that pertains to his/her job. Invariably as journals are reviewed in this manner, articles that seem interesting and relevant for work areas other than the specific topics of current interest for the senior researcher will be noted such that they can be subsequently copied and filed for future reference.

JOURNAL REVIEW FORM

Name of Journal: *Journal of Applied Behavior Analysis*

Topics Review for: *institutional staff training and/or staff management*

Number of Issues per Year: 4

Year	(1)	(2)	(3)	(4)	(5)	(6)	(7)	(8)	(9)	(10)	(11)	(12)
1987	___	___	___	___	___	___	___	___	___	___	___	___
1986	✓	✓	✓	✓	___	___	___	___	___	___	___	___
1985	✓	✓	✓	✓	___	___	___	___	___	___	___	___
1984	✓	✓	✓	✓	___	___	___	___	___	___	___	___
1983	✓	✓	✓	✓	___	___	___	___	___	___	___	___
1982	✓	✓	✓	✓	___	___	___	___	___	___	___	___
1981	✓	✓	✓	✓	___	___	___	___	___	___	___	___
1980	✓	✓	✓	✓	___	___	___	___	___	___	___	___
1979	✓	✓	✓	✓	___	___	___	___	___	___	___	___
1978	✓	✓	✓	✓	___	___	___	___	___	___	___	___
1977	✓	✓	✓	✓	___	___	___	___	___	___	___	___
1976	✓	✓	✓	✓	___	___	___	___	___	___	___	___
1975	✓	✓	✓	✓	___	___	___	___	___	___	___	___
1974	✓	✓	✓	✓	___	___	___	___	___	___	___	___
1973	✓	✓	✓	✓	___	___	___	___	___	___	___	___
1972	✓	✓	✓	✓	___	___	___	___	___	___	___	___
1971	✓	✓	✓	✓	___	___	___	___	___	___	___	___
1970	✓	✓	✓	✓	___	___	___	___	___	___	___	___
1969	✓	✓	✓	✓	___	___	___	___	___	___	___	___
1968	✓	✓	✓	✓	___	___	___	___	___	___	___	___

Figure 7. Sample of a completed *journal review form* used to organize screening of journals for specific topics of information. The check mark (✓) next to the issue indicates that the issue has been screened.

To help reduce the time and effort involved in the journal review process, an applied researcher can evoke the support of his/her staff research colleagues in the activity. Such assistance can serve as a nice opportunity for a senior researcher's agency co-workers to become more familiar with the professional literature as well as with applied research in general. With appropriate guidance, a senior researcher's colleagues within the human service agency can also assist in the actual reading and critiquing of the research articles. One means of providing the appropriate guidance in this regard (which is often needed due to the inexperience on the part of human service staff in reviewing journal articles) is to clearly specify exactly what type of information is desired from the articles. The specification can be enhanced through a form that requires the staff member who is reviewing the articles to answer certain questions that the senior researcher has determined as targeting the most relevant type of information to be acquired. For example, a form that proved useful for reviewing the behavioral research literature pertaining to methods of teaching self-care skills to mentally retarded persons is presented in Figure 8 (See Reid, Wilson & Faw, 1983, for the outcome of this particular review.) A form such as that depicted in Figure 8 not only facilitates the reviewing role of an agency staff member who may not be very experienced in critiquing research articles, it also helps to organize the process in that all reviewers are looking for, and providing, the same type of organized information. Organizing the information in this manner can facilitate an applied researcher's eventual task of summarizing, analyzing and/ or writing about the information in the literature.

Article Summary/Critique Format

1. Author(s) and Dates: *Nutter, D. & Reid, D.H. JABA 1978*

2. Summary statement of purpose: *Teach severely & profoundly retarded women to select color-coordinated clothing*

3. Participants (Number and MR level and special characteristics) *5 severely & profoundly retarded, ambulatory women*

4. Summary of treatment procedure: *simulation training w/ a puzzle of a woman; subjects were taught w/ instructions & feedback to color-match the clothes on the doll w/ probes taken using the actual clothing of the women*

5. Brief critique of research:

   Behavior definitions: *normal & abnormal matches — OK see #6*

   Observations and reliability: *good*

   Power of experimental design: *good—multiple baseline*

   Amount of behavior change: *good*

6. Special weaknesses or highlights: *+ observed community dress styles to determine norms of dress for the retarded woman; — however, never really measured the women's actual day-to-day dressing*

Other "Notes to Consider"

1. Make critique comments on <u>copy</u> of article.

2. Make record of relevant references.

3. Critique only experimental studies.

Figure 8. Sample of a completed *article summary/critique* form used to guide the critiquing of research articles for gleaning relevant informaion. In this sample, the form was used to obtain information from an article pertaining to teaching self-care skills to mentally retarded persons.

Writing Research Papers within a Human Service Job Role: A Difficult But Manageable Task

Earlier in this chapter it was noted that incorporating the writing of research papers into the routine job of an applied researcher is a rather difficult step in the multi-step process of conducting a research project in a human service setting. One reason offered for the difficulty was that many senior researcher type persons have not had adequate training in the technical aspects of writing research reports. Attempting to describe the technical skills necessary in this regard is certainly beyond the scope of this text. Nevertheless, a few key points will be discussed that seem particularly germane for persons attempting to write articles when operating within an applied job setting.

Sharpening a Practitioner's Technical Writing Skills

The goal in writing an applied research paper is basically to produce a manuscript that is: (a) easy to understand in terms of why a given investigation needed to be conducted, what occurred procedurally, what results were found and what the results mean; (b) concise in terms of providing only information that is necessary and; (c) hopefully, interesting. A clear technology for teaching researchers to write in such a manner does not seem to exist. However, one basic principle that can be especially helpful is, in essence, that *one learns to write by writing;* if a senior researcher wants to improve his/her proficiency in writing research reports, he/she should write as many such papers as feasible. Further, the papers (assuming, of course, that good applied research is being conducted to form the content of the papers) should be submitted to refereed journals for review. In this manner, not only will an applied researcher be obtaining practice in writing, he/she will be receiving feedback from journal editorial personnel that can be very valuable in terms of improving the researcher's manuscript-writing skills.

In applying the principle of improving writing proficiency by writing as much as possible, several steps can be incorporated by a senior researcher to enhance the quality of the writing *before* a given manuscript is submitted to a professional journal. For example, to aid in the organization of the content of an applied behavioral research report, L. Keith Miller's text *Reinforcing Research Behavior* (1977) can be quite useful. This text describes in very clear terms the main components of an applied behavioral research article and provides nice examples of how to structure what is written within each component. One word of caution, though, in using *Reinforcing Research Behavior* in this manner is that the text provides the structure for only the *basic* content of applied behavioral research articles; a senior researcher will need to elaborate considerably on the basic information suggested by the text. To help with the latter process, the best guide is to follow the organizational format of articles that have already appeared in the journal(s) to which the senior researcher is likely to submit his/her research manuscript for publication consideration.

Another helpful (actually essential) text for preparing applied research manuscripts is the *Publication Manual of the American Psychological Association* (APA), *Third Edition* (1984). Most journals that publish applied behavioral research papers require that the manuscript be prepared in APA format. Although the *APA publication manual* has a relatively tremendous amount of stylistic information (so much so that it is difficult for a reader to digest all the information), one of the most helpful components is the sample manuscript provided toward the end of the book. Before a manuscript is submitted to a journal, it can be very helpful for an applied researcher to compare a manuscript draft page-by-page with the sample provided in the *APA publication manual* as a last check to ensure that the appropriate format is followed.

In addition to using texts as just noted, a process that can be valuable in preparing a research paper is to have other senior researcher type staff critique the paper before the paper is submitted to a journal. Although this process usually requires several weeks' worth of time and a subsequent delay in submitting the manuscript, the end result in terms of improving the paper is typically worth the delay. In particular, it is helpful to study the comments of the reviewers in conjunction with each other. Almost invariably, where different reviewers independently note a problem with one part of a paper (even if the exact problem noted varies across reviewers), that specific part of the manuscript warrants some revision before submitting the paper.

Another suggestion in terms of writing a research manuscript for submission purposes is that the paper should be initially *written for journal reviewers*. That is, the first goal a paper must achieve is to convince journal reviewers (and subsequently the editor), that the manuscript should be published in the journal. Hence, the paper should be written with this goal in mind in contrast to the more final goal of convincing readers (i.e. the journal audience) of the merits of the research that the paper represents. Writing a paper for reviewers is somewhat different than writing a paper for the audience of the journal. Reviewers often need more detailed procedural information in the text about how a study was conducted than do the typical readers of the journal. Consequently, it is usually helpful to add more procedural detail in the draft of the paper that is first submitted to a journal relative to what usually appears in articles that are published in a journal issue. The rationale for this approach is as follows. First, editorial reviewers need to decide if, among other things, a study was conducted with sound experimental controls. To make such a decision, reviewers need to have a very good understanding of how an investigation was conducted, which requires a detailed description of the experimental procedures. When detailed procedural information is lacking, reviewers are more likely to assume that certain procedural safeguards were not employed. In short, it is usually better to make sure that a reviewer knows (or at least has ready access to) precisely what took place in an experiment, in contrast to letting him/her *assume* that something important did or did not occur.

When elaborating on procedural detail in a paper for the sake of reviewers, certain safeguards should be taken to include only necessary information. In particular, very lengthy, overwritten texts often have a seriously negative impact on reviewers. However, when a problem with excessive writing occurs, it is usually not with the procedural part of the paper. Rather, a frequent mistake made by inexperienced researchers is to overwrite the introduction and discussion parts of a manuscript. The latter sections are often overemphasized in an attempt by researchers to make the point that the research is very important and should be published. Such a process usually represents an "oversell" that is not very convincing for editorial reviewers. If the research did indeed address a relevant topic (Chap. 2), generally little elaboration is needed in the introduction and discussion. Journal reviewers are usually well versed in what constitutes an important research topic and can tell pretty quickly whether a paper addresses such a topic. In essence, a useful guideline in terms of what parts of a manuscript need to be elaborated on the most is to emphasize the "Methods" section of the paper. If the "Methods" section is not the longest part of the paper by far, then the paper probably should be rewritten. A good illustration of the relatively common mistake made by new researchers in overwriting non-essential parts of a manuscript is provided in the editorial correspondence in Appendix A regarding a paper submitted to JABA (see in particular comments of the Associate Editor and Reviewers A and D regarding unnecessary verbiage within the submitted paper).

In some ways it seems illogical that a paper would be written differently for journal reviewers and editors than for a journal audience. After all, it is the journal audience for whom the paper is intended in regard to disseminating useful information to a professional field, and it seems reasonable that the paper would be prepared specifically for whom it is primarily intended. Nevertheless, it is still the journal reviewers and editors who determine whether or not the journal audience will ever actually see the paper. Regardless, preparing a paper specifically for reviewers typically pertains to the submission draft of a paper and not as much to the final version that is published. If a journal accepts a paper for publication, the senior researcher can later edit out some of the procedural detail that was helpful for the reviewers but is probably not needed by the journal audience. Actually, it is common for reviewers to recommend that some of the procedural detail be omitted from the final draft that will be published once they have evaluated a manuscript.

Finding the Time to Write

As alluded to in the introductory comments to this chapter, a major difficulty in disseminating and publishing research while working in human service settings is incorporating manuscript writing into the routine job responsibilities. The primary problem in this regard is that it can be very difficult to find the time to write. Writing is probably the most difficult aspect of research to synthesize into the daily job situation in applied settings. The difficulty is due to the fact that manuscript writing is more different from typical agency responsibilities of a senior researcher than are the other aspects of conducting research. To illustrate, often the time spent in designing and conducting a treatment intervention as part of an applied research project to, for example, evaluate a new therapeutic approach to resolving a given client problem represents time that would need to be spent to help the client, regardless of whether or not a research project was involved. In this type of situation, the research activity that the senior researcher engages in is really no different (or only minimally different) than what would be required by his/her routine job duties. In contrast, writing a manuscript is not very similar to an activity that an applied researcher would routinely engage in during the normal work day or week.

Because of the difficulty in incorporating writing into a senior researcher's job in a human service setting, special care and planning are required to ensure that writing does indeed occur on a regular basis. This chapter section describes several procedures that can be helpful in accomplishing manuscript writing while working in a human service setting. Before describing such procedures, however, a point of clarification is in order: the procedures to be discussed refer only to the preparation of reports of applied research (i.e. journal articles), not to the preparation of books. For a variety of reasons (which really are not relevant to discuss here), writing book manuscripts requires a considerably different approach than preparing research articles for a practitioner who is employed full-time in a typical human service agency.

Organizing Writing Tasks to be Accomplished in Short Time Spurts. When considering a major writing task such as preparing a research manuscript for a journal article, researchers often tend to try to arrange relatively large blocks of uninterrupted time in order to concentrate on, and subsequently complete, a writing task. Such an approach may be quite beneficial for some authors, but it is usually rather fruitless for a senior researcher in a human service setting. Given the clinical, administrative and/or supervisory demands of a human service job, large periods of uninterrupted time during the routine workday are unusual. Of course, a senior researcher can undoubtedly arrange such times if he/she tries diligently enough, but to do so probably means that the researcher is neglecting important service responsibilities. Once again, such responsibilities *should never be sacrificed in order to do research*. Further, even in those rather isolated cases when a senior researcher can arrange the job routine to allow large periods of uninterrupted time for writing, doing so can have a negative impact on other agency staff members, because they *think* that the senior researcher is neglecting his/her job duties. As indicated earlier, it is well worth an applied researcher's time and effort to avoid, whenever possible, creating a negative impression on agency staff persons about any aspect of his/her research activity.

For the reasons just noted, manuscript writing should be conducted during relatively short periods of time (often no longer than one or one and a half hours) intermittently during the work-week. To successfully accomplish writing tasks in this manner, an applied researcher should initially outline major sections of a potential paper in a relatively detailed fashion. Once a planned manuscript is specifically outline, then it is much easier to write part of the manuscript during a short period of time. By having a detailed outline, the senior researcher can quickly begin writing a particular section of the paper without having to spend much time organizing his/her thoughts. Fortunately, in this regard, applied behavioral research articles generally follow a specific format that lends itself to careful outlining. (Table 3 lists the major parts of these articles and the interested reader is referred to Miller, 1977, for elaboration.)

Table 3

Outline for Applied Behavioral Research Articles

Major Heading	Subheadings
Introduction	
Methods	
	Subjects and settings
	Behavior definitions
	Observation sytem
	Interobserver agreement
	Experimental procedures
	Baseline
	Treatment conditions
	Experimental design
Results	
Discussion	

It can be especially helpful to take each article section and subsection as illustrated in Table 3 and make these the main parts of a manuscript outline *prior to* beginning the actual writing of the manuscript. Subsequently, shortly before writing any specific component that is listed in the outline, that respective component can in turn be briefly outlined. As just noted, this type of outlining process allows a senior researcher to quickly begin the actual writing of a particular manuscript section whenever an hour or so of uninterrupted time may arise during the workweek. For example, if a senior reseacher has scheduled an hour or two during the workday for an agency meeting and then the meeting is cancelled, by having a detailed outline ready the researcher can quickly refer to the outline and use the unanticipated "free" time to write a small section of the paper.

In using short spurts of time for writing manuscripts, a word of caution is in order: sometimes texts perpared in this manner appear somewhat disjointed, in that separate sections of the paper do not flow together very well. Indeed, because different sections are prepared intermittently across days and weeks, it is easy to write a manuscript section that does not relate well to a section that immediately precedes it in the paper, because the content of the preceding section is not well remembered by the writer due to the time delay between writing the two sections. To avoid this type of problem, once the basic sections of the manuscript (Table 3) are completed in draft form, subsequent editing and elaboration of the paper should be conducted during longer, uninterrupted periods of time (e.g. two to four hours). Editing the entire paper within one time span usually causes the disjointed aspects of the manuscript to stand out for the senior researcher, prompting him/her to make necessary revisions.

Identifying Opportune Times for Writing. Using the format just described in terms of accomplishing writing tasks within short spurts, a senior researcher can often schedule small blocks of time for writing during the course of the workweek. Even with short time blocks for writing, however, an applied researcher is likely to have a number of service-related interruptions (at least if he/she serves an important function within a human service agency). Hence, it is usually beneficial for a senior researcher to try to identify opportune times for writing that are relatively unlikely to have interruptions. There are several general time periods within many human service settings that are advantageous times for accomplishing writing tasks in this manner.

One time period that usually can be productive for writing purposes is Friday afternoon. In many human service agencies, Friday afternoon represents a relatively slow business time. A number of staff often take the afternoon off in order to have a long weekend and many staff, whether justified or not, seem to work at a very slow pace, frequently spending their time in non-work-related activities (planning or discussion the upcoming weekend, general socializing, and so on). Consequently, Friday afternoon is typically a time when fewer people will be calling on a senior reseacher for business-related reasons, frequently leaving several hours of time with a lower-than-usual probability of interruptions. Of course, for an applied researcher to use this time productively for writing, it is assumed that the researcher him/herself is indeed ready to work diligently on Friday afternoon in contrast to engaging in typical non-work activities as just described.

Similar to Friday afternoons, workdays surrounding holidays can also be productive times for accomplishing manuscript writing. Like Fridays, workdays close to holidays are usually slow work times in human service agencies, and a senior researcher's time is less likely to be as in demand as during more routine workdays. In particular, the period from late November through early January frequently can be an especially good time for a senior researcher to write research manuscripts. Not only do many staff take extra time off during this period, but a number of special holiday activities usually occur such that regular business operations are prohibited. Often, several hours for writing can be scheduled around the various holiday events during the workday. Again, however, if a senior reseacher is going to make optimal use of these slow business times to accomplish writing tasks, he/she must be willing to work somewhat diligently at times when agency colleagues are usually not so willing.

In addition to using typically slow times in human service settings in a productive manner, an applied researcher will often need to arrange other "low-probability-interruption" times for writing. In many ways, the times that will prove to be opportune will depend on the senior researcher's personal schedule and/or flexibility. For some individuals, working a flex schedule to allow one or two evening work periods during the week can be productive. Evenings are generally slower business times in most human service agencies than day periods. Early morning periods before the regular work schedule begins can also be productive writing times. Of course, working such schedules needs to be approved by a senior researcher's supervisor and needs to be accomplished without seriously jeopardizing more regularly scheduled work responsibilities.

A final approach to arranging low-probability-interruption time that warrants mentioning is scheduling time away from the agency work site for writing. Sometimes, applied researchers seek approval from their supervisors to stay at home or elsewhere in order to work on a research manuscript without distraction. This procedure is very risky if the time spent away from the work site is considered part of the senior researcher's actual workday. The risk is due to how other staff view such an activity, which is usually quite negatively. In short, being able to work away from one's work site is an unorthodox arrangement for the vast majority of working staff in human service settings, and if a senior researcher attempts to engage in such a process, he/she is usually asking for trouble from other staff. Agency staff most likely will view the researcher as being primarily interested in meeting his/her own professional needs at the expense of the service needs of the agency's clients. This point could be elaborated on (see also discussion in Chapter 2), but suffice it to say here that a crucial criterion for a successful applied research program is that a senior researcher not only needs to ensure that service obligations of his/her job are met but also that staff are aware that the senior researcher fulfills the routine job expectations. An applied researcher who spends work time away from the agency under the auspices of writing research manuscripts typically will not be meeting this criterion. This is not to say that writing should not occur away from the work site, just that writing should not occur as part of the senior researcher's compensated work time.

Using Self-Control to Ensure Writing is Accomplished. The strategies just described can be quite helpful in assisting an applied researcher in a human service agency to accomplish writing tasks. Nevertheless, because of the problems in incorporating manuscript writing into the routine of a human service job as described previously, this component of conducting applied research usually remains a difficult task for a senior researcher. Probably, the most important determinant of whether an applied researcher will overcome the various obstacles and consistently complete manuscript-writing tasks is the degree of self-control of the senior researcher: the researcher simply *must ensure that he/she writes on a regular basis*. Hence, it is generally necessary that an applied researcher spend a few minutes at the end of *each week* to evaluate how much writing has been accomplished. If a significant amount of writing has not occurred during the week—and certainly if *no* writing has occurred—then the senior researcher should take extra steps to make sure that some writing does take place the following week. In many ways, the longer a senior researcher goes without spending some time writing, the more difficult it is to later begin, or resume, writing.

There are several specific self-control strategies (e.g. see Goldfried & Merbaum, 1973, for elaboration) that can be used by a senior researcher to assist in ensuring that writing occurs on a regular basis. For example, for experienced and previously successful senior researchers, one method is to keep a record over months and years regarding when research manuscripts are submitted to journals for publication consideration. If such a record indicates that a longer-than-usual time period has surpassed without a manuscript being submitted relative to previous submission intervals, then the senior researcher should increase his/her current amount of time spent writing. On a more frequent basis, a senior researcher can maintain a weekly record of the amount of time spent writing or the number of manuscript pages completed. These types of self-monitoring practices can serve to heighten a senior researcher's awareness of his/her writing productivity as well as stimulate increased productivity.

Publishing the Manuscript

The final step in conducting a successful applied research project is publishing the manuscript in a refereed journal. This step entails submitting the paper to an appropriate journal to have the merits of the paper relative to it is publication worth decided by a small group of established researchers in the field (i.e. members of the journal editorial staff). As discussed in Chapter 6, one of the most rewarding events for a senior researcher is reading a letter from a journal editor which indicates that the senior researcher's manuscript has been accepted for publication. At that point all the hard work that was involved in planning and conducting the research project seems well worth the effort. Indeed, at that point it has been decided that the fruits of the researcher's labor will become a permanent product in history.

Determining Authorship

Publishing an applied research paper requires several actions on the part of the senior researcher beyond what has already been discussed. That is, once the project has been completed and the senior researcher has managed his/her time sufficiently to write the paper, several key decisions must be made. The first such decision is the authorship of the paper. Of course, if a senior researcher is to have a productive research program in a human service setting, he/she must collaborate with other staff members in the agency. Consequently, a decision has to be made regarding which of the collaborating staff persons should be listed first author, second author, and so on. Often, the decision regarding authorship is a very sensitive one. Many times, collaborators on a research project develop serious ill will among each other regarding the results of the authorship decision. Such ill will can be devastating for an applied researcher's future productivity, not to mention the fulfillment of his/her general service responsibilities within the agency. To avoid difficulties in determining the authorship of a paper, several guidelines can be helpful. The first guideline is the criteria for manuscript authorship established by the American Psychological Association (see APA publication manual referred to earlier). These criteria provide general rules by which authorship can be determined based on the relative amount of professional contribution of each collaborator in terms of designing, conducting, and writing the research project.

The second guideline regarding the determination of manuscript authorship pertains to the customarily perceived role of the senior researcher within typical human service agencies. Because the senior researcher is the most highly trained and skilled in research activities of all the agency collaborators on a research project, it is often assumed that he/she should always be the first author on a manuscript. Such an assumption not only contradicts the American Psychological Association's criteria referred to earlier, but, if put into action, the assumption can lead to serious difficulties among research collaborators. In particular, this assumption can lead to the deleterious "white knight" impression of the applied researcher within the human service agency (see Chap. 2). Actually, the senior researcher should *actively seek* to ensure that one of his/her agency research colleagues is usually first author on a manuscript. The rationale for such a recommendation is severalfold. First, if a senior researcher is going to have consistent success in applied research over the years, he/she must work with a number of colleagues and manage research projects such that one or more colleagues are conducting most of the procedural implementation components of the projects. In this manner, the senior researcher can have several studies underway simultaneously in contrast to if the senior researcher is doing the bulk of the work on one given project. Subsequently, if a colleague has conducted most of the professional work on an applied research project, then it is appropriate that he/she be the first author on the manuscript, not the senior researcher.

The second rationale regarding why a senior researcher should strive to allow an agency colleague to be first author on a research manuscript is due to the impact on the colleague. It can be very reinforcing for a colleague to be first author on a paper, especially if the colleague is well aware of the fact that he/she has worked diligently on a project and was instrumental to the project's success. As discussed in Chapter 6, a senior researcher must find ways to reinforce agency colleagues for their collaboration on research projects if the senior researcher is to maintain a productive research program. Reinforcing an agency colleague with (appropriate) first authorship not only aides the senior researcher's long-term research productivity by increasing the probability that agency staff will continue to be interested in collaborating on research, it can also help (albeit in a small way) the helping profession in general. Specifically, given the purpose of applied research of finding successful means of resolving important societal problems, the more skilled people (e.g. successful staff research collaborators) who are interested in participating in applied research on a consistent, long-term basis, then the more advances will be made toward resolving problems in the human services.

Another suggestion in terms of avoiding difficulties in determining manuscript authorship is really not a guideline per se but a point of clarification. Much of the ill will that is often generated among research colleagues, because a collaborator feels short-changed on the authorship decision, is somewhat ridiculous, because in the long run it does not matter very much whether an applied researcher is first or second author or whatever; what matters is that the researcher continues to publish good applied research from year to year as a (co)author. The importance of authorship order is frequently rather controversial among many researchers, but as viewed here, in actuality it is really more of an academic issue. If a researcher publishes good research on a consistent basis, regardless of ranking on authorship order, the researcher will have an impact on the human service field and his/her professional reputation will be appropriately enhanced. Further, in one sense, by reinforcing competent collaboration of other agency staff members by (appropriately) allowing such staff to be first authors on manuscripts, a senior researcher's impact can be significantly enhanced, because he/she will publish considerably more research over time due to the increased interest of staff persons in working with the senior researcher on future research projects.

A final guideline regarding the determination of authorship in order to avoid difficulties among research colleagues is to establish ground rules pertaining to authorship in the early stages of a research project. If the senior researcher explains to his/her colleagues at the onset of a project what the criteria will be for determining the authorship (assuming, of course, that the research will proceed somewhat according to plan and be successful in terms of the paper being submitted for publication), there is much less of a likelihood that problems among research collaborators will eventually develop. Although it is usually not certain exactly which collaborators will contribute the most to a research project prior to completion of the project and hence the exact order of authors cannot be initially determined, the *ground rules* by which the authorship will be decided should be initially discussed by the senior researcher.

Selecting a Journal

Once the authorship is finalized, then the next step for the senior researcher is to select a journal to which the manuscript will be submitted. Several variables should be considered in deciding on the appropriate journal. First, the audience of the journal should be considered in regard to whom will most benefit from the information in the manuscript. For example, some journals are intended for applied researchers (e.g.

JABA), whereas others are most intended for clinicians (*Education and Treatment of Children*); some journals are directed primarily at educators (*Exceptional Children*), whereas others are directed at managerial personnel (*Journal of Organizational Behavior Management*); some journals are aimed at persons working with developmentally disabled clients (*American Journal of Mental Deficiency*), whereas others are aimed at staff working with geriatric populations (*Journal of Behavioral Geriatrics*); and so on. Determining the target audience of a given journal can be decided in part by the information provided in the journal itself regarding its purpose. Additionally, a method of determining a journal's audience is to pay attention to the journals that one's colleagues and other professionals attend to in terms of what the latter have in their offices and/or say that they generally tend to read.

A second factor in selecting a journal, which is related to the first variable, is the type of articles that journals generally publish. Types of articles vary along a number of continua. One continuum is the subject population that the journal articles target. The journal, *Education and Treatment of Children,* for example, publishes articles with children and youth as the target participants, whereas the *Journal of Organizational Behavior Management* publishes articles pertaining to staff working in business and other organizational settings. A second continuum is the methodological focus of the journal. Because the orientation of this text is behavioral, the information presented here is aimed at applied researchers who are (or will be) involved in applied behavioral research. Consequently, the methodological focus of journals to which senior researchers should submit their papers should be at least partially behavioral. Fortunately, from the point of view of behavioral researchers who want to publish applied behavioral research, the availability of journals that publish applied behavioral investigations has increased dramatically since the late 1960s. Examples of the journals that publish a considerable amount of applied behavioral research are presented in Appendix B.

A third variable in selecting an appropriate journal for submitting a research manuscript is the criteria the journal editorial staff use to decide whether to accept or reject submitted manuscripts. Some journals clearly are far more stringent than other journals in terms of the required methodological rigor and social significance of the studies that are accepted for publication. In particular, for applied behavioral research, JABA is typically considered the most stringent journal.

Determining the degree of stringency of journals in regard to article acceptance criteria can be rather difficult unless a senior researcher has had experience in submitting papers across a variety of journals. Further, acceptance criteria within a given journal fluctuate to varying degrees across members of the journal's editorial staff (i.e. the stringency with which papers are reviewed varies depending on which members of a journal's editorial board review the paper). Nevertheless, a general idea about the experimental requirements of a journal can be obtained by: (a) comparing the methodological rigor among studies published in different journals and (b) discussing this issue with other applied researchers who have experience in working with various journals. A general guideline that may also be helpful is that new journals typically are less stringent with their manuscript acceptance criteria than are more established journals. Quite frequently, the former journals are seeking manuscript submissions relatively desperately, a factor that can enhance a new researcher's probability of success in publishing his/her research paper. This does not mean that new journals necessarily publish less-than-respectable papers, only that the newer journals are usually more likely to overlook minor problems with submitted manuscripts than are more established journals that have a larger number of papers submitted from which to choose which papers to publish. Irregardless, it is certainly more advantageous for a senior researcher (and especially a beginning researcher in a human service setting) to publish a paper in a new journal than not to publish the paper at all.

The Final Major Step: Sending the Paper to a Journal

Once all the steps in writing a research paper and determining the authorship and an appropriate journal have been completed, the next step is to actually send the paper to a journal. Each journal typically specifies in a given issue exactly what to send (e.g. how many copies of the paper), and the *APA Publication Manual* described earlier can also be helpful in this regard. However, one final step should be incorporated immediately prior to mailing the paper: the senior researcher should ensure that the final submission draft of the manuscript is the *very best* that he/she can prepare. Researchers often become anxious toward the end of a manuscript-writing task and want to complete the process quickly. This reaction is understandable when considering the tremendous amount of work that has been conducted since the original research idea was conceived, and that the researcher deserves to reap the benefits of the labor in terms of sharing his/her work through the publication process. Nevertheless, publishing research is a competitive operation where usually only the best research papers are published. In some ways representatives from a journal's editorial staff seem to employ a process of quantitatively comparing the good points and weak points of a given manuscript in attempting to determine whether or not to publish the paper. When there are problems in the preparation of a manuscript that could be corrected through a little more effort by the author (e.g. spelling mistakes, typographical errors, sloppy graphs), these problems extend the "weak point" list of the reviewer and can eventually impact the overall editorial decision. For any research project there will undoubtedly be some problems that an applied researcher cannot correct; no research undertaking is perfect. Hence, a researcher should not let the problem list with a paper be extended due to lack of a little final effort. In short, the senior researcher should not let his/her publication chances be diminished *to any degree* because of hurrying through the last phases of the research process and letting correctable problems with a manuscript go uncorrected. Delaying a few days or weeks in sending the paper to a journal is usually well worth the time spent to improve a manuscript with some final editing. In essence, ensuring that the paper is in the very best form that the senior researcher can prepare represents the final major step in successfully conducting an applied research project in a human service setting.

REFERENCES

Goldfried, M. R., & Merbaum, M. (1973). *Behavior change through self-control.* New York: Holt, Rinehart and Winston.

Miller, L. K. (1977). *Reinforcing research behavior: How to write articles for behavioral journals.*

Reid, D. H., Wilson, P. G., & Faw, G. D. (1983). Teaching self-help skills. In J. L. Matson & J. A. Mulick (Eds.) *Handbook of mental retardation.* New York: Pergamon Press, pp 429-442.

Whitman, T. L., Scibak, J. W., & Reid, D. H. (1983). *Behavior modification with the severely and profoundly retarded: Research and application.* New York: Academic Press.

Chapter 8

SUMMARY: THE KEY POINTS IN SUCCESSFULLY COMPLETING APPLIED RESEARCH

THE PRECEDING chapters have discussed methods of conducting applied behavioral research in human service settings. The procedures that have been described for successfully integrating research activities into the routine operations of human service agencies are both numerous and varied. Indeed, successful applied research endeavors require a practitioner to engage in many different types of activities. All things considered, however, it is not really expected that *all* of the recommended procedures for engaging in research activities will be implemented for each applied investigation that is conducted. Nevertheless, if a senior researcher is to have consistent success in conducting and publishing applied research as part of his/her work efforts in a human service agency, then at least *most* of the guidelines discussed in the perceding chapters should be adhered to *most* of the time.

Summarizing the key points regarding the guidelines for conducting behavior analysis research in human service settings without being needlessly redundant with information presented in preceding chapters is difficult. However, a brief review of the recommended guidelines may be helpful for a practitioner in terms of providing quick access to relevant information for planning and conducting an applied study. Consequently, some summary guidelines will be presented here. The recommendations will not be discussed in detail as such discussions have been provided previously; the interested reader is referred to the designated chapter accompanying each guideline for elaboration. For organizational purposes, the recommendations will be presented in accordance with the three main components that are integral in developing and maintaining a program of applied research: planning a study, conducting a study, and writing up a study.

Key Points in Planning an Applied Research Project

In planning an applied research project to conduct while working in a human service agency, a senior researcher should strive to ensure that:

1. Representatives from the agency's most competent pool of staff will be collaborating on the research endeavor (Chap. 3).
2. Agency staff who will be collaborating on the project have been involved in selecting the topic of research (Chap. 2).
3. The topic of research addresses an existing problem within the human service agency that needs to be resolved (Chap. 2).
4. The research question, when answered, will make a contribution to the professional literature (Chap. 2).
5. The senior researcher's supervisor has been informed regarding the planned study to a degree of specificity based on the supervisor's expressed interest (Chap. 4).
6. Available sources of external, supplemental research support have been considered and sought where appropriate (Chap. 4).
7. Guidelines for determining eventual manuscript authorship have been discussed with the staff research collaborators (Chap. 7).
8. If a multiple probe or multiple baseline design is to be used, at least three entities have been identified to allow ample opportunity for replication of experimental effect (Chap. 5).
9. An experimental design has been selected to allow for successive interventions if an initial intervention is ineffective (Chap. 5).

Key Points in Conducting an Applied Research Project

While conducting a study in a human service setting, a senior researcher should strive to:

1. Spend some time working on the ongoing project *each* day (Chap. 2).
2. Assist with any implementation aspect of the investigation on an as-needed-basis (Chap. 2).
3. Train and manage the involvement of agency staff collaborators such that there are backup persons to immediately replace a staff person who might be pulled away from a key implementation component of the study (Chap. 2).

4. Intermittently find ways to reward competent staff work on the research project (Chap. 6).
5. Continue the project until the dependent data indicate that the identified agency problem has been resolved, even if several interventions
   must be successively applied (Chap. 1).

Key Points in Writing an Applied Research Project

In writing the outcome of an applied research project in order to submit a manuscript to a professional, refereed journal for publication consideration, a senior researcher should ensure that:

1. Some time is spent writing a part of the paper at least *every week*
   (Chap. 6).
2. The format of the paper follows the guidelines of the *APA Publication
   Manual* as well as the organizational style of articles previously
   published in the journal to which the paper will be submitted for
   publication consideration (Chap. 7).
3. The manuscript is critiqued by several of the senior researcher's peers
   prior to the submission of the paper to a journal (Chap. 7).
4. The manuscript is not submitted to a journal unless every correctable
   problem with the paper has been addressed by the senior researcher
   (Chap. 7).

The guidelines just provided are by no means exhaustive of the criteria that usually need to be met if an applied researcher is to successfully
complete a research undertaking. Rather, the suggestions only highlight
some of the key elements that should be considered in attempting to
fulfill the dual mission of working as a practitioner — be it a clinician,
manager or administrator — *and* as an applied researcher in a human service setting. In this regard, the reader is reminded that for the most part
these guidelines (and most of the entire text) do not address the technical
aspects of research design and methodology. As discussed in Chapter 1,
although the technological aspects of applied research are crucial to the
success of a research endeavor, those aspects are not the primary concern here.

In addition to the key guidelines that should be adhered to in conducting applied behavioral research within human service agencies,
there are also some activities that should be avoided when possible.
Although no single activity in and of itself would necessarily prohibit
a research project's success, if these particular aspects of research

undertakings are not consistently avoided, they can make the task of an applied researcher much more difficult and/or unpleasant.

Key Activities that Should not be a Part of Applied Research Investigations

1. Experimental participants (staff and/or clients) should not be referred to as research "subjects" (Chap. 4).
2. The planned research should not be "over-talked" (Chap. 4).
3. Studies comparing different interventions generally should not be conducted, especially by new researchers (Chap. 5).
4. Where possible, the use of changing criterion experimental designs should be avoided (Chap. 5).
5. Reversal experimental designs should be avoided if withdrawing an effective intervention is likely to be harmful or the withdrawal is likely to be *perceived* as harmful (Chap. 5).

Two Most Essential Guidelines

All of the key points just summarized, as well as the related discussions as presented in the referenced chapters, should be helpful to a practitioner in a human service agency who is seriously interested in conducting applied research. However, of all the recommendations, two are by far the most critical. These two guidelines extend from the two basic premises of successfully conducting applied research in human service settings discussed in the introductory comments to this text. First, for an applied researcher to be successful, the *human service mission of the researcher's agency must be the first priority* of all his/her efforts, both research and non-research related. Although a given study or two can be conducted in a human service agency and result in a published journal article without really enhancing the agency's service provision, over the long run a researcher's investigative undertakings will not succeed if the research does not clearly assist the agency in fulfilling its human service mission. In essence, if a program of research does not overtly assist the human service agency in which the research is conducted to fulfill its mission of providing (and/or enhancing) client services, then there will simply be too many forces over time that counteract the research efforts to allow consistent success (see Chapters 1 and 2 for elaboration).

The second crucial component that must be adhered to if an applied researcher is to be successful in a human service setting is that he/she *must be willing to work very diligently.* In this regard, even if a number of the recommended guidelines discussed throughout this text cannot be followed in certain cases, a practitioner can successfully conduct applied research if he/she continuously and actively persists in working on research tasks. In many ways, what an individual must do in a human service setting to successfully conduct a program of applied research is analogous to what must frequently be done to provide *any* type of innovative change in service delivery systems. Robert Liberman has very adequately described the effort that is often required in order to affect innovative change in human service settings: a successful innovator "uses charisma, unflappable poise, humor, empathic assertiveness, a sense of timing, flattery, cajolery, persistence, bird-dogging, perceptiveness, and shrewdness" (Liberman, 1983, p. iii). In short, as with a successful innovator, the most important determinant of whether or not a practitioner will be successful at developing and maintaining a program of research in a human service setting is how hard he/she is willing to work and to persevere in trying different means of being successful.

The Challenge to Conduct Applied Research in Human Service Settings

This text began by attempting to build the case that if applied research in the human services is going to effectively and comprehensively fulfill its intended purpose of enhancing service delivery to people in need, then persons (i.e. practitioners) who are routinely responsible for providing those services should be integrally involved in research activities. There are undoubtedly many individuals in the helping professions, both researchers and non-researchers, who would disagree with such a strong view of the importance of practitioners being involved in applied research. In one way, the fact that the overwhelming majority of researchers who publish applied research related to the human services are affiliated with universities and not human service agencies (Chap. 1) is an indication of the common view of who should conduct research. However, there are also others who would make an even *stronger* assertion as to the importance of practitioners doing research than what has actually been presented in this text. One such view is that applied research should not be regarded as an activity that is ancillary to the role of human service practitioners but as an activity that is *expected* and *required* of professional practitioners. The essence of this view is that, by the nature of being a *professional* in the human services, a practitioner is routinely charged with attempting to provide the best services possible, and the only way to ensure that the best possible services are being attempted is to be continuously engaged in applied research that is aimed at evaluating and enhancing services. Further, practitioners should be required to conduct applied research because they are in the most advantageous position to resolve problems in human service delivery that applied research attempts to address; practitioners face the problems on a daily basis and are in the best position to control (at least relative to professionals external to the human service system) the contingencies and resources necessary to resolve the problems.

I will not go so far as to assert in this text that, in essence, practitioners are not fulfilling their professional obligations to the human services unless they actively participate in applied research. At this point, I would be simply pleased if those professional practitioners who have the basic know-how and desire to conduct applied, problem-solving research would be able to consistently engage in research activity and be supported in such endeavors. If indeed human service professionals can successfully conduct applied research within their day-to-day work situations, then the advances in the helping professions that are often reflected in the professional literature can be similarly reflected in the routine provision of services to clients in need.

REFERENCES

Liberman, R. P. (1983). Guest editor's preface. *Analysis and Intervention in Developmental Disabilities, 2/3,* iii.

APPENDIX A

A SAMPLE JOURNAL EDITORIAL
REVIEW PROCESS

THE REVIEW was conducted by members of the editorial staff of the *Journal of Applied Behavior Analysis* and pertained to a manuscript eventually published in that journal in 1977 (Reid, D. H., & Hurlbut, B., "Teaching nonvocal communication skills to multihandicapped retarded adults," Volume 10, p. 591-603). The editorial correspondence is presented verbatim as it was sent to the senior author, with the exclusion of some of the specific page number references to the original manuscript.

Letter from Journal Associate Editor to Senior Author of Submitted Manuscript

Dear Dr. Reid:

The manuscript "Teaching nonvocal communication skills to multihandicapped retarded adults" that you co-authored with Hurlbut is a fine example of applied behavior analysis. The problem is a socially significant one, the design and methodology is impeccable, and the results are clearly important to the residents who participated in the study. The four people who reviewed the manuscript provided their unanimous and enthusiastic support. My recommendation to the Editor is to publish a revised version of this manuscript in JABA.

The reviewers made many very helpful and useful comments about the manuscript. Many of these relate to a suggested reorganization of the manuscript. I especially liked the recommendation of Reviewer D to organize the manuscript into three experiments. I think this would add considerably to the clarity of the manuscript. Also, all four reviewers have detailed questions about the observation system that was used, the number of observers present to collect data and reliability, the position of the observers during the data collection, and so forth. These questions need to be answered in the revised version of the manuscript to enhance the replicability of the procedures that you describe. I have marked the comments and suggestions of the reviewers that I think are most important to include in the revision. I also suggest you attend to the specific and detailed comments that Reviewer D placed on the manuscript itself. These comments, I think, would help the understandability of the procedures that you have described.

In many cases the suggestions made by the reviewers will require lengthening the manuscript. However, the manuscript is currently much too long for the page limitations faced by JABA. Therefore, I suggest you reduce the length of the manuscript to no more than twenty pages of text. I think this can be accomplished by reducing the introduction somewhat and by greatly shortening the seven-page discussion in the current manuscript.

I will look forward to receiving three copies of a revised version of the manuscript very soon. Also, please return the manuscript that was marked by Reviewer D.

Thank you very much for making such a fine contribution to the field and for submitting your work to JABA. I will look forward to hearing from you soon.

Sincerely,

Dean L. Fixsen, Ph.D.
Associate Editor

Comments of Reviewer A

The authors are to be commended for an excellent research project. This article is clearly written, as all aspects of the methodology and results are well explained. The writing style is excellent and few grammatical errors are present. The area of research is definitely a difficult one and, consequently, the results are impressive. The population of subjects in the study may not be of substantial interest to some JABA readers; however, considering the clear methodology, results, and generalization measures that were taken, I believe the article definitely deserves publication. Below are a few changes that should be considered:

1. Table 1 can be eliminated.
2. The first sentence on page 4 does not make sense to me.
3. In Phase I, Reliability is reported before Experimental Design, whereas Experimental Design is reported first in Phase II. The same order should be used in reporting methodology across phases.
4. On Page 8, it is unclear how many observers were present when reliability data were collected. It sounds as if two observers were present during all sessions. Did one of these two collect reliability data, or was an additional observer present on reliability-collection days? Also, the method of calculating reliability is unclear. Was a response by response check used to determine agreements and disagreements between observers, or was the total correct (or incorrect) responses for one observer compared to the total number for the second observer? Please clarify. Hopefully, the former method was used.
5. On page 13, second sentence, I assume a test session always followed a training session. If so, it would help for the authors to directly say so. Also, if so, what was the time span between training and test sessions?
6. On page 24, the authors state that a minimum of five correct responses (42%) on five consecutive sessions was the criterion level of accuracy for proceeding to the next phase. This should be reported in the "Method" section rather than in the Discussion.
7. The length of the manuscript should be reduced. The introduction and discussion are probably the best places to trim down the length.

Most of these comments are relatively minor. I believe the authors have done an excellent job in designing a study and writing the paper. My congratulations!

Comments of Reviewer B

It was a most pleasant task reviewing the manuscript entitled "Teaching non-vocal communication skills to multihandicapped retarded adults" submitted by Reid and Hurlbut. The communication problem dealt with is of critical importance, the procedures appear to be most practical, and the results very believable and encouraging. The contribution it will make to the field will no doubt be most significant. In sum, this manuscript has all of the elements that make publication in JABA an absolute necessity.

It is clear that considerable thought and effort went into the preparation of this manuscript. I have made notations and offered some suggestions on the manuscript itself. In addition to the notations provided, I have a number of questions pertaining to several aspects of the study that I hope the authors will consider in preparing a revision.

Observation System

The description of the positioning of the observers is somewhat difficult for this reader to visualize, especially given the distances between the residents and the communication board (15-20 inches). From the description it seems that the observer in front would be right on top of the board. Would it be more accurate to state that one observer stood behind the resident's recliner and the other off to the side approximately one to two feet away from the resident? Also, were both observers always present or just for reliability assessments?

The description of the training sequence is extremely clear and detailed. If the data are available, it would be interesting if the authors could indicate on Figure 1 the point at which manual guidance was faded for each of the patients. It would also be helpful for the reader to know the approximate number of training sessions needed for each resident for both experiments. To facilitate replication, it would be useful for the reader to know if there was a formal criterion for terminating coordination training (i.e. able to point to two consecutive blocks without assistance).

The reliability figures that are presented in the text are somewhat difficult to follow. I believe that the table reporting the means and range of scores for each resident for each experimental condition would suffice along with a summary statement something like the one suggested at the bottom of page 13. The discussion of reliability on page 21 also needs clarification and a breakdown of the level of observer agreement for both the baseline and the training conditions, since the point is to show that the measurement procedure was consistent over time. Some suggestions are offered in the text (p. 21) for making the summary of reliability figures more concise.

To avoid puzzling the reader, the explanation of why Victor did not participate in Experiment II should be included somewhere before the discussion of the results on page 22, perhaps as an opening sentence under identification training (p. 17).

In the presentation of the experimental conditions, I think it would be easier to follow if a chronological order was maintained. That is, generalization tests might best be described *after* the training and before discussion of follow-up sessions for ease in understanding.

The inclusion of the volunteer staff to test the resident's communication skills was a lovely inclusion in Experiment II. As described, however, it seems to provide more a measure of the validity of the changes in behavior than a true test of generalization, especially since the question form was altered and the contingencies differed from the original testing condition (either of which might have affected the outcome). I think that it would be more appropriate to discuss this test in a section of social validation emphasizing the interpretability of the communication response by strangers.

In the discussion the authors, I feel, have provided the reader with a fair yet cautious interpretation of the results and with an excellent discussion of the implications of these findings. The paragraphs in the section dealing with the post-training (maintenance) phase of Experiment II and the reliability of the measurement system, however, seem more appropriate to include in the "Procedure" section.

In summary, this is an exciting piece of research that should generate much needed additional research in the area of functional communication skills for retarded persons. I hope that the authors will continue to carry out the careful, innovative research that is illustrated by this manuscript and to pursue their interest in this most critical area.

Comments of Reviewer C

The manuscript "Teaching Nonvocal Communication Skills to Multihandicapped Retarded Adults" submitted by Dennis H. Reid and Bonnie Hurlbut is clearly a demonstration of socially significant research with a unique, frequently overlooked population. The manuscript reports the results of a two-phase teaching program designed to teach functional communication skills to adults previously unable to interact with their environment. In addition, this manuscript points out that the teaching program, utilizing specially designed apparatus, can be integrated into an institution's daily routine.

Institutional staff working with similar populations would no doubt be eager to attempt replicating the described treatment. However, the manuscript as written does not provide adequate detail for replication. It is the opinion of the reviewer that the manuscript be accepted pending the inclusion of suggested revisions. The primary reason for this recommendation involves questions regarding information provided in the "General Methods" section (pages 5-9) and in Phase I and II "Methods" and "Results" sections.

I. General Method Section

1. A detailed description of individual subjects is given in the "General Method" section. However, the reader is not told why the ward staff recommended these residents over other similar residents. To replicate the procedures with the appropriate population, it would be necessary to know if the ward staff were told to make their recommendations according to specific criteria (e.g. age, sex, handicap, IQ).

2. Additional information regarding the setting appears to be needed. "Living wards" no doubt are not consistent across institutions. A description of the social climate (e.g. number of other residents and staff present, noise level, competing activities) should be reported.

3. Although very specific definitions of the behaviors (e.g. correct, incorrect) are given, a number of important observer and observation procedure details are not reported. Specifically, observer selection, observer training and recording procedures are not sufficiently well described to permit replication. Separate sections should be included to describe how observers were selected (e.g. from the institution's staff, college population) and how they were trained (e.g. who did the training, length of time it took, materials used). Recording procedures are described within the "observation system" section, however, some confusion still exists. For example, it is not clear whether there is more than one observer present during test sessions or if observers are present during training sessions. A step-by-step description of the exact recording procedures would rectify this problem

4. Information absent in the description of observer selection and training also is absent in the description of the coordination and identification trainer. It is extremely important for the reader to have this information, since the trainer has the primary responsibility for teaching the communication skills. Details such as trainer background (e.g. education, occupation), training procedures (i.e. How was the

trainer taught to implement the treatment procedures?) and length of time needed to train the trainer should be included.

5. In spite of the extensive reference to the reliability of the measurements used, some questions still remain regarding the procedures used. Exactly how did reliability checks occur? Were observers told when a reliability check would occur? Were observers given feedback regarding reliability? Who was the second observer during reliability checks? Answers to these questions would supply the needed detail.

In general, the above comments involve reorganizing and expanding the format and information already provided. A reorganization of the format is given below which may assist in responding to the suggested revisions.

    I. Subjects and Setting (include description of resident selection, description of residents, description of setting)
    II. Observer Selection and Training
    III. Observation Procedures (define the behaviors, recording procedures et al.)
    IV. Trainer Selection and Training
    V. Reliability (details of procedure and calculation)

The suggested revision of Phase I and II "Methods" and "Results" sections involve, for the most part, expanding and clarifying information already provided.

II. Phase I: Method and Results Sections

1. In describing the procedures used during the experimental conditions, it is not clear how many observers were present during test sessions or who conducted the test sessions (e.g. trainer, experimenter). This information should be stated specifically.

2. In addition to reporting the average number of test sessions per condition per resident, the number of days test session occurred per resident and how soon after training sessions testing occurred should be reported. The number of test session days per resident could be given within the descriptive part of the report (as indicated in the margins of the manuscript) or shown on Figure 1.

3. Including the average number of training sessions per resident and the number of days training occurred should be specified.

4. An additional piece of information would be useful in clarifying the reported reliability. It is stated that at least three reliability observations were conducted for each experimental condition for each resident. During which condition(s) and for which resident(s) did the three reliability observations occur? This information could be included in Table 1 (as noted on the submitted manuscript).

III. Phase II: Method and Results Sections

1. In the description of the "Leisure areas," it is mentioned that residents were more sccessful in pointing to certain areas of the communication board than others during coordination training. This is the first reference to this finding. It is important to either mention this earlier (e.g. Phase I Results) or explain more fully at this point.

2. Three earlier suggestions regarding Phase I apply to Phase II: (1) the number of observers present during a test session, (2) the number of days each experimental

condition encompassed, and (3) how soon after a training session testing occurred. This information could be mentioned either in the descriptive part of the report, included on the graph (Fig. 2), or both.

3. A table showing reliability data for Phase II (as given for Phase I reliability data) should be provided for further clarification of the reported reliability.

IV. Discussion

1. In the "Discussion" section the exact number of times one disagreement between observers resulted in a reliability calculation of zero should be stated.

Suggestions for minor revisions are given within the margins of the manuscript.

Again, the authors are to be commended for the apparent social significance of the research. Applied research of this nature which could potentially improve the lives of institutionalized adults is obviously of importance to the field.

Comments of Reviewer D

This article is a very nice demonstration of a technique to teach non-vocal communication skills to multihandicapped retarded adults. In my opinion, this has been a sadly neglected area. The procedure described in this manuscript will allow persons with limited hand or limb control to learn to communicate with others in their environment. The article is particularly interesting due to its appeal for the rights of handicapped persons in the fields of communication and recreation. In addition, the studies are methodologically sound and the results are encouragingly successful. Thus, I would like to recommend the manuscript be published in JABA, provided certain revisions be made by the authors.

In general, I found the manuscript to be well and clearly written. Nevertheless, it is unnecessarily long, owing to some repetition and a concentration on detail. My suggestions for shortening the manuscript are written in the margins throughout my copy. Other suggested revisions are as follows:

1. I believe the manuscript would be most clear in a format of three experiments. The first experiment would be the same as Phase I. The second experiment would include identification training and generalization, and the third experiment would include the "social validity" or "Does it work with strangers?" phase. In such a format, each experiment should have its own "Method" section and "Results and Discussion" section. In the latter section, the discussion should be limited to one or two paragraphs containing the conclusions and any qualifications. At the end of the article would be a "Discussion" section for the whole study, which would not repeat any of the information previously covered but which would present qualifications for the procedure as a whole, relate the research results to previous literature, and provide ideas for future research.

My reasons for the three-experiment format are twofold. First, the second phase of training is rather confusing, as it now includes three different procedures and three sets of results. Secondly, the training procedure seems to fall naturally into three steps: (1) coordination training, where the resident learns to point to areas on the board; (2) identification training, where the resident matches a verbal cue, "library," to the picture of the library; and (3) choice training, where the resident learns to respond to the question, "What would you like to do during free time today?" Since all of the residents correctly responded to what might be a pretest for choice training, this type of training was not needed. Perhaps, the ward aides did this choice training by asking the residents what they would like to do each day and then escorting them to the recreation place of their choice. It's unfortunate (and a weakness of the study) that this was not documented by the authors. Such "training" may be a necessary component of the total procedure, but it is unclear when the "choice test" was given to the residents in relation to this training.

Nevertheless, the test information provided for this step of training yields the needed social validity measure to answer the question, "Can the residents not communicate with strangers?" A positive answer to this question is, after all, the goal of the study. Perhaps the authors might include a brief description of what could be done to teach residents choice behaviors if they cannot communicate with strangers when the test is given.

2. Under the "Procedure" sections, the contingencies operating during training should be specified more clearly. Praise (and a description of the types of praise used) should be mentioned whenever it was used. Were refreshments only used during baseline, or were they included later during training? What kinds of refreshments were used?

3. The procedures for test sessions should have their own headings. This will avoid the confusion I initially experienced in understanding the study. Condition titles should be changed accordingly (see Figures), since they are really test-session results that are reported and not training-session results. Baseline sessions should only be called "baseline sessions" to avoid confusion with later test sessions.

4. Quite a lot of reliability results are reported for a seemingly simple procedure. In my opinion, these sections can be cut down considerably, especially if a table is included. One matter that concerns me is the report of means across reliability checks. I would prefer a report of the total number of agreements over the total number of trials (230 agreements on 300 trials) along with the resulting percentage figure (77%) for each resident. Since the results for correct and incorrect trials are fairly comparable, the authors might mention this in a sentence and report only total agreement measures.

5. The final discussion might include some ideas for different types of communication that may be taught with the procedures. For example, they might mention other types of questions to which the residents could respond using a similar device. In addition, they might describe the need for procedures to train residents to initiate and maintain "conversations" and ask questions. Another interesting possibility is communication between residents. Since ward aides have little time to "converse" with each resident, it would be super if residents could be taught to converse with each other.

In conclusion, I would like to congratulate the authors of this manuscript on a fine job. The study represents a positive contribution to an area which has been neglected in the past, and I am happy to recommend that it be accepted for publication after the necessary revisions have been made.

APPENDIX B

EXAMPLES OF JOURNALS THAT PUBLISH APPLIED BEHAVIORAL RESEARCH

INFORMATION regarding the scope and content of the journals has been drawn from descriptions provided specifically within each respective journal. The first section of Appendix B presents samples of journals that publish behaviorally oriented papers exclusively, predominantly, or at least on a relatively frequent basis. The second section presents samples of journals that periodically publish applied behavioral articles, although that is not the primary focus of the journals. Rather, the latter journals focus on applied specialty areas as indicated in their respective titles. In essence, one option for publishing applied behavioral research is to seek journals such as those exemplified in the second section that represent a given speciality area in a human service field in which a particular behavioral investigation was conducted. The journals presented are only a small sample of potential publication outlets in specialty fields.

SECTION 1

Journals Covering a Variety of Content Areas
(publisher in parentheses)

Behavior Modification (Sage Publications)—publishes relevant research and clinical papers in the general area of applied behavior modification; includes papers on assessment and modification techniques for problems in psychiatric, clinical, education and rehabilitation settings as well as among normal populations if there is a clear analogue to the applied setting; accepts single-case experimental research and group comparison designs if they present particular clinical interest; considers review papers and theoretical discussions if they contribute substantially to the application of behavior modification.

167

Behavior Therapy (Association for Advancement of Behavior Therapy) — publishes original research of an experimental and clinical nature that contributes to the theories, practices and evaluation of behavior therapy or behavior modification; considers methodological and theoretical papers as well as evaluative reviews of the literature; occasionally publishes case studies if the treatment or problem is novel.

Journal of Applied Behavior Analysis (Society for the Experimental Analysis of Behavior) — publishes original reports of experimental research involving applications of the experimental analysis of behavior to problems of social importance; considers technical articles relevant to such research and discussion of issues arising from behavioral applications.

Journal of Behavior Therapy and Experimental Psychiatry (Pergamon Press) — publishes original papers in behavior therapy and experimental psychiatry; includes descriptions of therapeutic methods and case reports in an attempt to bridge the training gap in behavior therapy for medically trained therapists; focuses on research involving new procedures, theoretical discussions of behavior disorders in particular and behavior change in general, and change in neurotic, psychotic and psychopathic behavior.

The Behavior Therapist (Association for Advancement of Behavior Therapy) — emphasizes *rapid* publication of news and articles relating to the broad field of behavior therapy; includes high-quality case studies, communications, technical reports and research reports, as well as discussion papers providing provocative and topical content.

The Behavior Analyst (Society for the Advancement of Behavior Analysis) — publishes general-interest articles on theoretical, experimental, and applied topics in behavior analysis; includes articles on the past, present, and future of behavior analysis, as well as its relationships with other fields; also publishes literature reviews, discussions of previously published work, or reinterpretations of published data; does *not* accept basic or applied experimental studies with original data.

Behavior Research and Therapy (Pergamon Press) — focuses on papers that apply learning theory to the understanding of the acquisition and extinction of behavior disorders; includes applications to psychiatric and social problems, experimental research relating learning theory to maladaptive behavior and "high-level" theoretical papers.

Child and Family Behavior Therapy (Haworth Press) — focuses on behavioral applications and methodology with children and families; includes experimental and discussion papers.

Advances in Behavior Research and Therapy (Pergamon Press) — publishes extended reports and reviews of research in the theory and practice of behavior therapy; focuses on encouraging and facilitating the dissemination of new ideas, findings and formulations in the field; emphasizes longer papers, in that each issue is made up of either one major paper of about 35,000 words or two shorter related papers; includes papers that critically review a topic, present a systematic theoretical analysis or any integrated series of experiments, or a combination of these three types of presentation; preference given to papers that attempt to relate the theory, methods and results of experimental psychology to behavioral and emotional problems and their modifications.

Journals Focusing on Developmental Disabilities

American Journal of Mental Deficiency (American Association on Mental Deficiency) — publishes original contributions to knowledge of mental retardation and the characteristics of mentally retarded persons, including reports of empirical research, tightly conceived theory papers, and systematic reviews of research literature on specific aspects of mental retardation. Literature reviews must be incisive, comprehensive, and critical; in general, preferred approach is objective, scientific, experimental, and theory-oriented; program descriptions, anecdotal case reports, applications of research findings, description (without evaluation) of techniques or procedures, and personal accounts are not accepted; reports of evaluative research on new treatment methods may be accepted if there is evidence of proper design and implementation.

Research in Developmental Disabilities — new journal formed by merging previous *Applied Research in Mental Retardation* with *Analysis and Intervention in Developmental Disabilities* (Pergamon Press).

Mental Retardation (American Association on Mental Deficiency) — publishes applied articles including new teaching approaches, administrative tools, program evaluation studies, new program developments, service utilitization studies, community surveys, public policy issues, training studies, case studies and reseach studies that emphasize the application of new methods.

Journal of the Associaton for Persons with Severe Handicaps (The Association for Persons with Severe Handicaps) — publishes articles which report original research, authoritative and comprehensive reviews, conceptual and practical position papers which offer new directions, and effective assessment and intervention methodologies and service model program descriptions.

Education and Treatment of the Mentally Retarded (Council for Exceptional Children) — publishes papers focusing on the education and welfare of retarded persons; includes research and expository manuscripts as well as critical literature reviews; focuses on identification and assessment, educational programming, characteristics, training of instructional personnel, habilitation, prevention, community understanding and provisions, and legislation.

Journals Focusing on Miscellaneous Topics

Education and Treatment of Children (Clinical Psychology Publishing Company) — devoted to papers on the development and improvement of services for children and youth; primary criterion for publication is direct value of information to educators and other child care professionals for improving their teaching/training effectiveness; publishes original experimental reports and replications, program descriptions, research reviews and issue-oriented papers.

Behavioral Residential Treatment (John Wiley & Sons) — publishes reports of research involving the utilization of behavioral techniques in residential treatment environments; including papers on behavioral strategies related to assessment and treatment of clients as well as behavioral assessment/evaluation, training and management techniques used with staff; accepts research articles, brief reports, literature reviews and discussion articles.

Journal of Abnormal Child Psychology (Plenum Press) — focuses on behavioral pathology in childhood and adolescence; publishes papers on research and theory; priority given to empirical investigations in etiology, assessment, treatment in community and correctional settings as well as educational settings, epidemiology, prognosis and followup, pharmacological intervention and ecology of abnormal behavior; target populations include persons with neurotic and organic disorders, delinquency, psychosomatic conditions, and behavior disorders accompanying mental retardation; includes some significant brief reports.

Journal of Behavioral Medicine (Plenum Press) — focuses on papers aimed to improve understanding of physical health and illness through the knowledge and techniques of behavioral science, including topics on prevention, treatment and rehabilitation; specific topics of interest include adherence to medical regime and health maintenance behavior, self-regulation therapies, biofeedback for somatic disorders, and study of appetitive disorders (e.g. alcoholism and smoking); publishes experimental studies, theoretical and review papers, technical and methodological papers, case studies.

Journal of Organizational Behavior Management (Haworth Press) — publishes papers on the application of behavior management in business, government, and service organizations; original research articles emphasizing the advances in the knowledge of applied behavior analysis in work and organizational settings; includes studies reporting effects of various reinforcers in the work setting; implementations studies; studies of feedback effects; research of self-management procedures in the work setting; and studies of operant procedures on the variables of productivity, absenteeism, turnover, efficiency, job satisfaction, or other work-related behaviors.

Behavioral Assessment (Pergamon Press) — publishes papers in the areas of assessment, design, methodology, statistics, measurement, and program evaluation regardless of population or setting; includes: reports of original research that employ experimental, correlational, or simulation methodology and utilize either within- or between-subjects design; review or discussion articles that are based on experimental data and that have theoretical, conceptual, or applied implications; and case studies which emphasize measurement or design.

SECTION 2

Samples of Journals in Specialty Human Service Fields that Periodically Publish Applied Behavioral Research Relating to the Area Reflected in the Respective Journal Titles

Addictive Behaviors (Pergamon Press)
Therapeutic Recreation Journal (National Recreation and Park Association's National Therapeutic Recreation Society)

Journal of Music Therapy (National Association for Music Therapy)

American Journal of Community Psychology (Plenum Press)

American Journal of Occupational Therapy (American Occupational Therapy Association)

Exceptional Children (Council for Exceptional Children)

Journal of Mental Deficiency Research (Blackwell Scientific Publications, England)

Journal of Physical Education (National Physical Education Society)

Behavioral Disorders (Journal of the Council for Children with Behavioral Disorders)

Journal of Autism and Developmental Disorders (Plenum Press)

Journal of Rehabilitation (National Rehabilitation Association)

AUTHOR INDEX

SUBJECT INDEX